PREPARING FOR POWER

A Critical Study of the History of the British Working-Class Movement

by

J. T. MURPHY

with a new introduction by

JAMES HINTON

and with the original Foreword by

SIR STAFFORD CRIPPS

PLUTO PRESS LONDON

First published 1934
This edition published 1972 by arrangement with Jonathan Cape Ltd

ISBN 0 902818 22 8 (hardback)
ISBN 0 902818 23 6 (paperback)
cover designed by Robin Fior GRR
Printed in Great Britain by
Redwood Press Limited, Trowbridge, Wiltshire

PREPARING FOR POWER

CONTENTS

CONTENTS

CONTENTS

CONTENTS

INTRODUCTION
TO THE SECOND EDITION

John Thomas Murphy was born in 1888, the son of a blacksmith's striker. His family was poor, not least because of his father's drinking bouts and habit of leaving the smithy fires for an alcoholic tramping holiday for several weeks each spring. From the age of seven, Murphy combined school with hawking bread and cakes baked by his mother and selling milk for a local farmer. At thirteen he went to work at Vickers' Brightside works in Sheffield, became an apprentice, and remained there, in later years a shop steward, until 1918. A teetotaller and an earnest nonconformist, Murphy decided to go in for the Civil Service examinations when he was eighteen, but was forced to abandon this ambition at the last moment when his father was sacked, and he became prematurely the family's chief breadwinner. He remained studious, but his attention turned from theology and preparing for the Civil Service examinations, to philosophy and revolutionary literature. He read Marx, Connolly and others whilst turning propeller shafts at the Brightside works.

Shortly before the war Murphy's name first appears in the working-class press as secretary of both the Amalgamation Committee and the Herald League in Sheffield. He played an important part in the establishment of the shop stewards' movement in that city, and by 1917 was recognised as a national leader and theorist of the movement.

Murphy wrote *Preparing for Power* shortly after leaving the Communist Party in 1932. In it he focuses on a crucial period in the history of the British working-class movement—the pre-war syndicalist upsurge, the wartime shop stewards' movement, and the immediate post-war years.

In building local Workers' Committees based on the workshops and independent of trade union officialdom, the shop stewards' movement was able to fuse and transcend the two antagonistic traditions from which its leaders had emerged—the Socialist Labour Party's 'dual unionism' which wrote off the existing unions as rotten props of the capitalist order, and the Amalgamation Committee Movement's purely propagandist approach which sought to transform the existing unions into revolutionary industrial unions from within. It was Murphy above all who, in a pamphlet *The Workers' Committee* (1917), developed and expounded the novel theory of independent rank-and-file organization, first proclaimed by the Clyde Workers' Committee in the autumn of 1915:

> 'We will support the officials just so long as they rightly represent the workers, but we will act independently immediately they misrepresent them. Being composed of Delegates from every shop and untrammelled by obsolete rule of law, we claim to represent the true feeling of the workers.'

The leaders of the shop stewards were not able to draw the full revolutionary implications of their war-time actions until after the war, when the movement's power was already in decline. It was only in 1919 that Murphy developed a critique of trade union officialdom, and a strategy for transforming the 'passive' strike into the 'active' struggle for power which closely paralleled ideas put forward by Lenin in *The State and Revolution* and Antonio Gramsci in his writings on the Turin factory sit-ins. Fired by the revolutionary optimism of that year,

Murphy went beyond the concept of rank-and-file independence to the idea of the dictatorship of the proletariat and the seizure of state power by the Workers' Committees (or Soviets). This 'sovietist' theory was new. It identified as the agency of working-class power something which had no place in either of the major traditions of the time: the reformist orthodoxy, central to which was the effort to take control of the existing state machine by winning a majority in parliament, and the syndicalist strategy, which, neglecting the inevitably defensive role of trade unionism within capitalist society, envisaged a Congress of Industrial Unions as the main agency of a transition to socialism. Armed with his sovietist theory, Murphy played a leading role in the negotiations for Communist Unity during 1919. In 1920 he went to Russia as a delegate from the shop stewards' movement.

Murphy's trip to Moscow was a turning point in his political development. When he arrived he was, as he put it in his autobiography *New Horizons*, 'a young provincial skilled workman with a clear-cut theory of how society could be reorganised under the control of the workers'. At the time, 'none of us saw the political party as anything other than a propaganda body for the spread of Socialist ideas'. But after reading *'Left-Wing' Communism, an Infantile Disorder*, after seeing the Bolshevik Party in action and talking to Lenin, he was convinced, with the blinding force of revelation, that there was a need to construct a revolutionary party capable not only of preaching socialism, but also of leading the working class in the fight for soviet power.

While Murphy was gaining this understanding he was simultaneously losing something of his previous grasp of the importance of the workers' own, independent activity.

(This is reflected in this book in an underestimation of his own role as a theorist at the time.) This was not a result of some inner logic of Leninism; rather, it grew out of the general situation of the revolutionary movement in Britain in the 1920s.

When he left for Moscow, the shop stewards' movement was already in decline. Unemployment, which followed the armistice, and systematic victimisation of militants in the engineering workshops had undermined the workshop power on which their organisation had rested in wartime. The whole theoretical structure of 'sovietism' erected on the experience of that power, was threatened. The theory of the revolutionary party, instead of emerging on a rising tide of mass activity, started out in Britain as to some degree, a substitute for that spontaneity. It proved impossible to build a party based—as Bolshevik theory insisted it be—on the independent rank-and-file organization of the workers in the factories.

Murphy's journey to Moscow was symbolic, too, of another feature of British Communism. His ability was soon noticed by the Russian leaders of the new International and he was co-opted onto its central organs—first in the Red International of Labour Unions, and later on to the Executive Committee of the Communist International itself. In all he spent nearly half of that critical decade in Moscow, becoming more and more detached from the working-class struggle in Britain. He became a leading supporter of Stalin's bloc in the International during the fight with Trotsky, and returned permanently to England only at the end of 1928—as one of the most vociferous advocates of the ultra-left 'New Line', insisting, against all the evidence, that the working class was moving rapidly towards a new revolutionary offensive. Eventually, sickened by the sectarianism he had done so much to promote, Murphy left the Party. He moved rapidly rightward through the Socialist League and the Popular Front agitation of the later 1930s and died, aged 77 in 1966.

Murphy's critique of the Communist Party which he had helped to found is a radical one—the Party should never have been formed. 'Had the [Second Congress of the International] examined the situation in each country and decided upon the formation of communist parties in those countries where the internal position of the working-class movement was ripe for such a decision . . . it would not have thrust upon small immature groups of communists the tasks and responsibilities of independent parties and made it easy for the reactionaries to thrust them into isolation.' So long as the Party operated in effect as the left wing of the Labour Party and the trade unions its situation was a tolerable one, and its members were able to make a significant contribution to the labour movement. But when, with Murphy's temporary approval the Party swung sharply to the left, effectively liquidating both its left-wing support in the Labour Party and the Minority Movement in the unions, the basic contradictions in its policy became apparent.

There is no need to accept Murphy's analysis in order to recognise that the questions he raised then are still important. Was the Party's sectarian isolation after 1929 the inevitable consequence of its formation in a period of declining working-class combativity? Or was it the result of avoidable tactical errors? Murphy blames the sectarianism of the British revolutionary tradition for the fact that 'only in great moments of struggle which of themselves generate revolutionary opinions has the influence of revolutionaries spread. When the critical stages have passed and the fervour of the struggle has receded then they have lost ground again.' But can one expect a revolutionary party to be anything more than a sect in the absence of mass working-class activity on its own account, of spontaneous working-class revolt?

Murphy's own political evolution stands witness to the impasse of revolutionary socialism in Britain fifty years ago. Naturally our evaluation of it today is different from his. Yet his account in *Preparing for Power* still remains what it always was, a living testimony and a superb history of the British working-class movement during the first quarter of this century.

JAMES HINTON,
Leamington, August 1972.

PREFACE

In view of the fact that the writing of this book marks a great change in my political outlook, I venture to preface a few personal observations which may assist the reader more easily to appreciate its purpose and significance.

My introduction to politics was through my trade union – the Amalgamated Society of Engineers. My first acquaintances in this union were syndicalists of the amalgamation committees. I became a shop steward, a local official of the union, and later played a prominent part as a leader of the Shop Stewards' and Workers' Committee Movement in England during the war period. My first introduction to a political party was through the late Arthur MacManus, a leader at that time of the Socialist Labour Party and later the first chairman of the Communist Party of Great Britain. I joined the Socialist Labour Party and quickly became a member of its executive committee. When it merged with the British Socialist Party and others and thus formed the Communist Party I went with it and in 1921 became an executive member of the Communist Party. I remained in the leadership of that Party until I resigned from it in May 1932, following a dispute on the question of the Party's attitude to the demand for British credits to and trade with the Soviet Union, to which policy it was opposed.

The pros and cons of the dispute are of little moment now. Suffice it to say that I regard that dispute, and the many disputes which had preceded it, as part of my evolution away from the sectarianism in which I had been nurtured from the earliest days of my entrance into politics.

PREFACE

Immediately I left the Communist Party I found myself in a position of complete political isolation. I had, from the moment of my entering into party politics, endeavoured to steep myself in the history of the working-class movement and Marxism, and to expound a working-class policy. But I now realized that whatever contribution I had to make to working-class politics had been given to parties which were nothing more than sectarian groups on the fringe of the working-class movement.

Instead of organizing a body of opinion within the Labour movement and seeking to transform it in the process of its evolution, the Communist Party became an oppositional body. The ferocity of its criticism and challenge as an alternative party, antagonized the workers to revolutionary theory and strengthened the hands of the reactionary and conservative elements within the Labour movement.

I therefore determined on a re-study of the history of the working-class movement and Marxism. The first result was my decision to join the Labour Party as the mass political party of the workers, to subscribe even to what I regard as errors and mistakes, confident that the dynamics of the class struggle will force the revolutionary changes necessary to the fulfilment of the historic destiny of the working class.

The second result is the critical review of the British working-class movement contained in these pages. I hope it will help others to see that the actions of the masses are more important than a hundred resolutions and correct statements of this or that doctrine.

I must here express my sincere thanks to Mr. F. W. Hickinbottom, Sir Stafford Cripps, Sir Richard Rees, Mr. J. F. Horrabin and Mr. J. Middleton Murry, who read the book in manuscript and made many helpful criticisms and suggestions. Especially do I acknowledge my indebtedness to Sir Stafford Cripps who, in addition to the above, readily undertook to write his thoughtful foreword to the book.

J.T.M.

Who is it speaks of defeat?
I tell you a Cause like ours
Is greater than defeat can know;
It is the power of powers!

As surely as the earth rolls round
As surely as the glorious sun
Follows the great world moon-wave,
Must our Cause be won!

What is defeat to us?
Learn what a skirmish tells
While the great Army marches on
To storm earth's Hells!

Songs of the Army of the Night –
FRANCIS ADAMS

INTRODUCTION

No class ever appears on the stage of history fully conscious of the tasks to be thrust upon it by the process of social evolution. It emerges from the darkness of immaturity only through long and difficult struggles, often frustrated by changes in the situation over which it has no control. Especially is this true of the working class – the modern proletariat.

It is the product of social evolution corresponding to a definite stage in the development of the forces of production of capitalism. It becomes conscious of itself as a class, and of its historical purpose, and becomes transformed into the class ready to take the future into its hands as a result of countless struggles with its class enemies.

This transformation is possible only by the fusion of scientific socialism with the working-class movement. Mass struggles, revolts of a hungry and persecuted class, do not of themselves guarantee revolution. Only when they are harnessed, organized, led and directed by a scientifically equipped leadership that has transformed the spontaneously developing movements of revolt into revolutionary conscious, and politically enlightened, forces of social revolution, is the proletarian revolution possible.

Scientific socialism is not a direct product of the working class. Contradictory as it may seem, scientific socialism emerges from the development of bourgeois science and philosophy. Capitalism could not develop without at the same time spreading scientific knowledge. From the ranks of the bourgeois intelligentsia came the discovery of the laws of social development by Karl Marx, the son of a lawyer, ably assisted by Frederick Engels, a capitalist manufacturer. Lenin, himself a product of the bourgeois intelligentsia, says of socialism,

> 'The theory of socialism grew out of the philosophic, historical and economic theories that were elaborated by the educated representatives of the propertied classes, the intellectuals. The founders of scientific socialism, Marx and Engels, themselves belonged to the bourgeois intelligentsia.'[1]

Hence, unless these two forces – scientific socialism and the mass struggles of the proletariat – come together, there can be no socialist victory. This victory, however, depends not only upon the degree of the development of the power of the working class, but also upon the stage reached in the decline of the system it is destined to overthrow.

The wage earning class of this country, though the oldest, was not the first victorious proletariat. That honour fell to the proletariat of Russia in its seizure of power in November, 1917. This was not due to some peculiar inherent qualities of the Russian workers as compared with the workers of the rest of the world, but to the fact that, arriving later in history, and crystallizing within itself the experience of the international proletariat in the party led by Lenin, it broke the fetters of international capitalism at their weakest link.

Capitalism in Russia was overwhelmed with the dead weight of a rotten aristocracy and landlord class. It had been drawn into the vortex of the world war of 1914–18 utterly unequipped for so mighty a conflict. It was a backward agricultural country. Its industry was in its

[1] *Collected Works*, vol. iv, p. 115.

infancy and quickly proved incapable of waging the war of steel and iron. Its long frontiers, stretching over thousands of miles of varied territory, demanded means of support it could not give. Millions of workers and peasants were dragged into such desolation, and the army was plunged into such devastating defeats, that the inevitable breakdown of the whole system presented the proletariat with its historic opportunity. It seized that opportunity, and, in alliance with the peasantry, began the building of the new order of socialism.

The proletariat of this country has a longer history precisely because British capitalism has a longer history. British capitalism is more powerful and possesses far greater powers of resistance than Russian capitalism. The British working class is faced with a correspondingly greater task of conquest. As yet the British workers have had no such opportunity as the Russian proletariat to deliver the final blow to capitalism, although they have already delivered blows that have shaken it to its foundations. The working class, however, has still much to learn and the disintegration of the old order has to reach a much more severe stage of crisis before the final blow can be delivered. It is the aim of this book to show the evolution of the British working class, from its origin in the industrial revolution of the eighteenth and nineteenth centuries to the present period of capitalist crisis, as a class *preparing for power*.

There are clearly defined stages in British history when the working class marches forward as a class. There are periods when all revolutionary aims are submerged and almost forgotten, when, in the midst of a prosperous and expanding capitalism the proletariat itself shares the 'spoils of prosperity' and thinks in terms of capitalism, regarding it as a permanent order of society and itself as a 'co-partner' in that society.

But such a stage inevitably passes and the class struggle inexorably reveals itself as an inescapable law of social development inseparable from society based upon private property relations. Once again the revolutionary ideas emerge and new movements appear expressing the new phase of working-class evolution which finally penetrate deeply the working class as a whole.

These phases have been treated by all the constitutional historians as aberrations in the process of adaptation to the existing system. The writer, however, sees in these movements not aberrations and deviations from the 'normal' development of society but the evidence of coming fundamental changes in the direction, form, and content of the struggles of the working class. More attention is therefore given to them in these pages than most other writers of British working-class history have been willing to give.

Revolutionary Marxism has already established with scientific accuracy both the laws of social evolution and the conditions historically necessary for the working class to become the ruling class. The writer, therefore, has not attempted in this book to expound these views but rather to show how they are being fulfilled, especially with regard to the evolution of the working class itself.

The section of the book dealing with the war period of 1914–18 deals a little more fully with the history of the shop stewards' movement because of the entire absence of anything but the most cursory accounts of its struggles, despite the fact that these struggles were rich with new experiences.

At the same time the writer does not lay claim for the

book as a whole to be more than a critical outline. The working-class movement in Britain is only at the beginning of its new revolutionary phase and has yet to produce the army of revolutionary critics and investigators which are necessary to examine the rich history of the class struggle of the oldest of the proletariats and to do justice to the hundred and fifty years of its travail. But as an outline the writer hopes it will do good service in the cause of preparing the working class for power.

CHAPTER I

THE INDUSTRIAL REVOLUTION

THE modern working class is the direct product of the Industrial Revolution of the latter half of the eighteenth and the first half of the nineteenth centuries. This period is universally recognized as the epoch of industrial capitalism, of the development of machine production and large scale industry, and the formation of the two principal classes of modern society, namely, the bourgeoisie and proletariat – the propertied capitalist class and the propertyless working class.

These two classes co-exist. Neither can exist without the other. Neither fell from the sky. Both were the direct products of society already divided into classes.

Feudalism preceded capitalism. It was a more primitive form of society with its lords of the manor, its vassals, guildsmen, journeymen, serfs, etc. But however poor the 'lower classes', they were not excluded from all ownership.

Feudal production and exploitation were based upon the division of the soil amongst the greatest possible number, under the domination of the feudal lord. The lord was rich according to the number of people under his domination working the soil and rendering him its products.

The serf was part owner, if only a tribute paying owner of the land attached to his house and co-possessor of the common land. Unlike his predecessor the slave, he could not be sold. He belonged to where he was born.

The serfs could emancipate themselves either by running away and becoming journeymen, or handicraftsmen, or buying their freedom by money payment to their overlord and becoming peasant proprietors. During this period (fourteenth century) England was passing through a slow process of transformation from serfdom to a system of free farmers. The great revolt of the serfs known as the Peasants Revolt ended serf labour and established free farming England. According to Macaulay in the period following the revolt there were 'not less than 180,000 proprietors, who, with their families must have made up more than one-seventh of the population deriving their subsistance from little freehold estates'.

Industry was handicraft industry. The workers owned their own tools and were organized in guilds composed of masters and journeymen. The journeymen were the men who later became masters.

The spinning jenny invented by Hargreaves in 1764 set the pace towards the new machine factories which shattered this domestic economy for ever. The industrial revolution had begun.

A whole series of names tell the story of the remarkable change in the mode of production which followed. Watt, Arkwright, Wedgwood, Stephenson and hundreds more, proclaim the change which made England the Workshop of the World. It was not long before Macaulay, the historian of capitalism triumphant was able to write

> 'Our fields are cultivated with a skill unknown elsewhere, with a skill that has extracted rich harvests from moors and morasses. Our houses are filled with conveniences which the kings of former times might

have envied. Our bridges, our canals, our roads, our modes of communication fill every stranger with wonder. Nowhere are manufactures carried to such perfection. Nowhere does man exercise such a dominion over matter.'[1]

That, however, was only one side of the picture. Hand labour went through a most painful extinction. Mr. and Mrs. J. L. and Beatrice Hammond describe the position of the working class of this period most vividly:

'The depreciation of human life was the leading fact about the new system for the working classes. The human material was used up rapidly; workmen were called old at forty; the arrangements of society ensured an infinite supply; women and children were drawn in, and at the end the working class, which is now contributing not only the men but the entire family, seemed to be what it was at the beginning, a mere part of the machinery without share in the increased wealth or the increased power over life that machinery had brought . . . it had degraded the work-people to be the mere muscles of industry. Men, women and children were in the grasp of a great machine that threatened to destroy all sense of the dignity of human life. . . .'[2]

Thus the whole economic and political life of the country was completely changed. Handicraft industry was swept away and in its stead came the revolutionary technique of machine industry, the division and

[1] *The Town Labourer*, p. 1. [2] Ibid, pp. 35-6.

subdivision of the labour process, social methods of production in place of individual methods of production.[1]

The first reactions of the working class to the new conditions consisted of violent protests against the new inventions and appeals to return to the 'good old days' of domestic serenity and cottage industry. These protests were classified as Luddism, because a man named Ned Ludd initiated this form of protest by destroying a stocking frame. The first law against the destruction of machinery and factory buildings was passed in 1769, but in March, 1812, Parliament passed a law for the protection of machinery, punishing with death those found

[1] According to Porter's *Progress of the Nation*, and official data quoted at length by Engels, the imports of raw cotton rose from 5,000,000 pounds in 1771 to 528,000,000 pounds in 1841. 76,500,000 pounds of woven cotton goods were exported in 1834.

'The chief centre of the industry is Lancashire, where it originated: It has thoroughly revolutionized this country, converting it from an obscure, ill-cultivated swamp into a busy lively region, multiplying its population tenfold in eighty years and causing giant cities such as Liverpool and Manchester, containing together 700,000 inhabitants and their neighbouring towns – Bolton with 60,000, Rochdale with 75,000, Oldham with 50,000, Preston with 60,000, Ashton and Stalybridge with 40,000, and a whole list of other manufacturing towns to spring up as if by a magic touch.' –*Conditions of the Working Class in England in 1844*, p. 8.

A similar transformation took place in the West Riding of Yorkshire. 75,000 pieces of woollen cloth were produced in this district in 1738, but in 1817 the quantity had risen to 490,000 pieces. 101,000,000 pounds of waste were worked up in 1801. This rose to 180,000,000 pounds by 1835. 3,400 tons of flax were imported in 1814, rising to 19,000 tons in 1833. 4,300 tons of iron products and 4,600 tons of pig iron were exported in 1805. In 1834 the whole of the iron products had risen to nearly 700,000 tons of which 107,000 tons of pig iron were exported.

The population of towns increased enormously. Bradford increased its population from 29,000 in 1801 to 77,000 in 1831, Halifax from 63,000 to 110,000, Leeds from 53,000 to 123,000. Sheffield increased from 46,000 in 1801 to 110,000 in 1844. Birmingham from 73,000 to 200,000.

The demand for agricultural products increased so greatly that between 1760 and 1834 not less than 6,840,540 acres of waste land were reclaimed and England was transformed from a grain exporting country to a grain importing country.

A thousand miles of roadway were built between 1818 and 1829, while responsible for practising Luddism. In June, 1813, eight workmen were hanged at York for this offence.

This first protest movement of the proletariat cannot be classified as revolutionary. It was in fact, so far as its economic aim was concerned, reactionary – an attempt to turn history back upon itself. It was not the machinery that was the enemy of the proletariat but the system of ownership which turned it to account as a means of the shameless exploitation of the proletariat. Luddism was, however, only one early phase of working-class revolt.

In 1792 there was founded the London Corresponding Society. Its founder was Thomas Hardy, a Scotch shoe-

in Scotland between the years 1803 and 1844, 900 miles of roadway and 1,000 bridges were built.

Remarkable changes took place in the development of the classes and the distribution of wealth. Arthur Young gives an estimate of the distribution of occupations and national income prior to the industrial revolution as follows: In 1770 the population was about 8,500,000. Of these 3,500,000 were agricultural, 3,000,000 in the manufacturing industries, 700,000 in commerce, 200,000 in the professions, 500,000 military and officials, 500,000 were paupers.

The total national income is given as £119,000,000. Of this amount agricultural population take £66,000,000, manufacture £27,000,000, commercial £10,000,000, the professions £5,000,000, military and officials £5,000,000. Interest on capital £5,000,000.

According to Colquhoun the population had risen to 17,000,000 by the year 1812. The wealth produced in that year he says amounted to £430,000,000. Of this the higher and lower nobility numbering with their families 416,000 persons received £58,000,000; the yeomanry with their women and children numbering 1,400,000 persons received £40,000,000; the merchant class totalling 194,000 persons received £27,000,000; shopkeepers (700,000, including their families) received £28,000,000; the manufacturers, including their families, totalled 264,000 and received £35,000,000; the agricultural population, including their families, labourers and miners, totalled 3,154,142 persons, received £33,400,000 or £11 per head; 4,343,389 industrial workers, mechanics, artisans and their families received £49,000,000 or approximately £11 per head. There were 1,647,900 persons classified as paupers. The amount spent on poor law relief rose from £1,250,000 in 1760 to £7,847,000 in 1818. Thus the social pyramid was complete – a relatively small propertied landlord and capitalist class at the top concentrating the greatest proportion of the wealth into their hands and a growing propertyless class at the bottom, poverty stricken, pauperized and oppressed.

maker working in London. Its leader was John Thelwall, a poet and journalist. This society, which was composed principally of leaders, received its inspiration from the French Revolution. It made contact with the French Convention and the United Irishmen, when the latter were busy preparing for insurrection.

This society was suppressed by the Corresponding Act of 1799 which prohibited all communication between political societies. Nevertheless it had done enormous work and was really the first step towards *a workers' political organization* in Britain. It did much to focus attention on the social wrongs of the period and to set forth definite political demands, including Universal Suffrage and the Rights of Labour. Hence quite early in the history of the proletariat the question of the *extension of the franchise becomes an important feature of its agitation.*

This question played such an important part in the subsequent struggles that it is of interest to observe how it happens so. It is perfectly clear from the outset that it was not conceived as a tactical measure related to some larger revolutionary strategy. Such a consideration came later, in the history of the Chartist movement.

A number of important reasons forced this question into the foreground. The working class had no experience of any other form of government than parliamentary government. It had no political party and therefore no programme. It had no organization, no press, no popular education. It felt the power of the government over it. Petitioning the government of the day was the customary method of people with a grievance to be remedied by Parliament and became the popular form of mass agitation and protest. The absence of cheap newspapers and the general illiteracy of the population also made the organization of petitions the natural means of mass activity. The extension of the franchise aimed to supersede the petitioning of Parliament.

But another factor entered into the situation which made the question of the extension of the franchise into a popular issue. The need of the rising capitalist class, the product of the industrial revolution, to have political power commensurate with their economic power exercised considerable influence on the situation.

Parliament was at this time the exclusive monopoly of the landlords and colonial interests. The propertied interests in the rural areas, which were in process of being denuded of their population, exercised the vote, whilst the new towns produced by the industrial revolution were unrepresented.

These were the elements which created the basis for the tremendous mass movements of this epoch culminating in the Reform Act of 1832, the repeal of the Corn Laws in 1846, the Chartist agitation up to 1849, the Ten Hour Act and the first Factory Acts.

Before the movement for the extension of the franchise and the birth of the Chartist Movement, however, a more elementary movement was born – namely, the Trade Union Movement. Writing of this movement, Marx says:

> 'The great industry masses together in a single place, a crowd of people unknown to each other. Competition divides their interests. But the maintenance of their wages, this common interest which they have against their employer, unites them in the same idea of resistance – combination begins. . . .'

At first combinations were usually created during the progress of a strike. By 1810 large strike movements were taking place with cotton spinners and miners in the forefront of the struggle. They fought not only for higher wages, but for factory regulations for female and child labour.

All these battles were conducted in the teeth of fierce government repression. The form of organization waging the struggles was largely that of the trade union which developed a widespread federated activity. It was this mass activity, leading to the growth of class loyalty and solidarity on the part of the workers, that was the driving force behind the parliamentary generalship of Francis Place and Joseph Hume for the legalization of trade unions.

Francis Place, like many others, did not understand the part he was playing in the history of the class struggle. He did not understand that he was at the head of a class liberation movement, striking off fetters of oppression that would enable it to march forward with greater confidence and organized power. He thought he was assisting in the *destruction of combination*! Writing to Sir Francis Burdett in 1825 he wrote, 'Combination will soon cease to exist. Men have been kept together for long periods only by the oppression of the towns, these being repealed, combination will lose the matter which cements them into masses, and they will fall to pieces. All will be as orderly as even a Quaker's Demise . . .![1]

Instead of the trade unions disappearing, the repeal of the repressive legislation was the signal for a great advance of the workers, the growth of all forms of combinations, trade unions, national associations, attempts to form a union of all the unions, etc. It paved the way to the popularization of the sympathetic strike, the extension of the small local strike to the General Strike.

[1] Webb's *History of Trade Unionism*, p. 109.

This struggle to transform sporadic and spontaneous actions into permanent organized actions that could consolidate achievements and prepare future actions, spread into all industries including the agricultural industry.

It was quite natural therefore, when the great impetus came for the organization of trade unions on the repeal of the Combination Laws in 1824, that the agricultural labourers should play a great part. The trial and transportation for seven years of the Dorset Labourers for administering the oath of loyalty to the trade union is one of the best known events of early trade union history.

Following these savage sentences tremendous demonstrations of protest were organized. A quarter of a million signatures were obtained to a petition demanding their release. Over 100,000 workers marching behind trade union banners demonstrated in London.

During 1829 and 1830 hunger riots took place all over the country. Machines were wrecked, ricks were burned, workhouses were destroyed and strikes were numerous. The trade union movement was therefore born and grew in the midst of a tumultuous period of struggle of the whole working class.

The passing of the Reform Bill of 1832 by no means succeeded in allaying the storm. The first actions of the new government following the passing of the Reform Bill incensed the workers. Whatever assistance there was for the workers in the old Poor Law was now taken away. The Government practically wiped out all relief. The class war was intensified.

The most revolutionary leaders of the workers' movement had warned the working class against the Reform Bill, but the popular will prevailed. The disillusionment was all the greater and the anger of the workers at the gross betrayal of all pledges and promises aggravated and inflamed the economic struggles which had given rise to the trade unions.

It was this gross betrayal of the workers by the middle class, that for the first time gave widespread popularity to anti-parliamentarism of the syndicalist type and to schemes for the abolition of Parliament.

Although there was little clarity as to the form of government to supersede parliament, two tendencies were apparent. Owenism was one. It conceived of a new society coming through the union of the classes, i.e. class collaboration. Robert Owen, the great pioneer of this scheme, proposed the organization of Industrial Productive Co-operatives and Consumers Associations, of great educational schemes and the abolition of the difference between town and country by the trade unions buying land and establishing agricultural co-operatives. These ideas, of course, were far in advance of the machine breakers. They did not attack machinery. They attacked the question of the ownership of the machines and struck hard against the whole conception of the private ownership of the means of production.

The other tendency was definitely class war syndicalism. This was led by James Morrison and Smith. The former was an operative builder, the latter was the son of a weaver. They began as supporters of Owen but broke away from him because of his class collaboration theories. Their position was stated with great vigour in the pages of the *Poor Man's Guardian.* They said, 'These reports show that an entire change in society – a change amounting to a complete subversion of the existing "order of the world" – is contemplated by the working classes. They aspire to be at the top instead of at the bottom of society – or rather that there shall be no bottom or top at all.' Again they said in the *Crisis*, 'We have never yet had a House of Commons. The only House of Commons is a House of Trades and that is only just beginning to be formed. We shall have a new set of boroughs when the unions are organized; every trade shall be a borough, and every trade shall have a council of representatives to conduct its affairs. Our present commoners know nothing of the interests of the people. They are all landholders. How can an employer represent a workman? There are 133,000 shoemakers in the country, yet not one representative have they in the House of Commons. According to the proportion they bear to the rest of the population they ought to have twenty-five representatives. The same is with the carpenters and other trades in proportion. Such a House of Commons, however, is growing. The elements of the Reformed Parliament is now blasted, and like the character of a woman when lost, is not easily recovered. It will be substituted by a House of Trades."[1]

These two leading tendencies gave a great impetus to the growth of the unions and were responsible for the project known as the 'Grand National Consolidated Union' which had enrolled in 1833, according to the press of the period, not less than 800,000 workers. Owen wanted this instrument for the peaceful establishment of the New Society of Co-operation. The others, waging a daily class war of strikes and demonstrations, visualized an extension of these strikes into the general strike, a universal folding of arms, which, by bringing production to a standstill would paralyse the capitalist class and

[1] *Crisis*, April 2nd, 1834. *History of British Socialism*, by M. Beer.

enable the workers to take control of industry. Benbow has the credit of being the pioneer of this theory of the general strike. It was not to be the preliminary to insurrection, but the alternative to insurrection.

Instead of the many and varied disputes growing into the general strike they remained local, draining the Consolidated Union of its funds. This was due to the lack of centralized authority and the variety of issues which gave rise to the local strikes. The local unions decided the strikes. The Central Council of the Grand Consolidated approved but it was the approval of many strikes and not the merging of the many into a single strike with one issue, for which the workers as a whole were prepared to fight. Hence the drainage of central funds and the collapse of the Grand Consolidated within a year. But the local unions survived for they were rooted in the daily experiences of the workers.

During this period the Chartist movement was born. The Chartist movement did not arise because the workers were disillusioned with the results of the economic struggles. It would be much nearer the truth to say that the Chartist movement represents the answer of the working class to the political betrayals of the middle class by the Reform Act. The fight for the Charter was conceived by the workers as a fight to achieve power in order to attain the social aims of the working class.

The actual beginning of the Chartist movement did not wait upon the collapse of Owenism and Syndicalism. The first steps were taken even before the passing of the Reform Bill, although Chartism only became a mass movement with the growth of the disillusionment following the Reform Act. On May 25th, 1831, there was established in London 'The National Union of the

Working Classes'. It set out its aims and object as follows:

1. To avail itself of every opportunity in the progress of society, for the securing for every working man the full value of his labour and the free disposal of the produce of his labour.
2. To protect working men against the tyranny of the masters and manufacturers by all just means as circumstances may determine.
3. To obtain for the Nation an effectual reform in the House of Commons of the British Parliament, annual parliaments, extension of the suffrage to every adult male, vote by ballot, and especially no property qualifications for members of Parliament.
4. To prepare petitions, addresses and remonstrations to the Crown and both Houses of Parliament . . . etc.

This organization became the London Working-men's Association in 1836 and the demands outlined in clause 3 of the above programme, became the basis for the famous Charter. 1836 was marked by a great trade slump which increased the difficulties of the economic struggles of the workers. But the fighting spirit was undimmed. The Chartist Programme was sent to 150 working-men's clubs during 1837. It caught on. It pointed a way forward. Demonstrations of enormous size took place all over the country. The demand for people to arm was a commonplace and to many meetings the people came armed. There was no doubt about the class character of the movement or its militancy and revolutionary intentions.

The Government fought back. Torchlight processions which had been a feature of the demonstrations were declared illegal. National organizations were also made illegal. Arrests, trials for treason, the imprisonment of leaders were frequent.

Manchester became the great storm centre of Chartism after its demonstration of 100,000 people in the autumn of 1838. From this great meeting were elected the first delegates to the Charter Convention, held in London in 1839.

This convention of fifty-three delegates opened on February 4th, 1839. It was divided into two principal groupings, a division which continued throughout the history of Chartism. One group stood for the use of physical force as the means to achieve the Charter. The other group believed that the end could be achieved by moral persuasion.

It is of importance to observe the social composition of this movement. At no time was it a compact proletarian mass. It was composed of industrial workers, of impoverished home workers, artisans, agricultural labourers, the new 'aristocracy' of the craft unions, some intellectuals and middle-class radicals.

The two latter elements dominated the London Working-men's Association led by Lovett. These favoured the policy of class collaboration and declared the aim of the association to be, 'to win equal political and social rights for *all classes of society* by the use of legal means'.

The physical force group was led by O'Connor and O'Brien in its early stages, and by Ernest Jones and Harney in the later period. They were bitterly opposed to class collaboration. 'Don't believe those who tell you that the middle and working classes have one and the same interest,' said O'Brien in the *Poor Man's Guardian*. 'It is a damnable delusion. Hell is not more remote from heaven, fire more averse to water than are the interests of the middle to those of the working classes.'

It is clear also that this section was more concerned about the *struggle for the Charter* than the Charter itself. They were convinced that the Charter would not come by legal means but only through civil war. At the same time they were not clear as to the kind of government that was to take the place of Parliament, except that it should be one with working class content.

It was not until the later stages of Chartist history that the question of physical versus moral force became the decisive issue. When Harney put the question to the Convention, 'What is it proposed that we do if Parliament refuses to grant the Charter?' the Convention side-stepped and decided not to discuss the question. Meanwhile it prepared the campaign for a monster petition to be sent to Parliament.

On May 13th, 1839, the Convention removed to Birmingham. Here it had again to face the question raised by Harney. O'Brien declared that the Convention was not in a position to recommend energetic measures. The Convention urged the refusal to pay rent and taxes, the withdrawal of savings bank deposits and the declaration of a general strike developing into armed insurrection. It proceeded only with its peaceful measures, and when it reassembled on July 1st the Government had decided on repressive measures.

Workers demonstrations were broken up. Numerous arrests were made. Martial Law was proclaimed in Birmingham and the provocative actions of the Government were such that the houses of well-known enemies of Chartism were burned to the ground. But the Convention appeared to be powerless. Divided against itself it did not even attempt to call the great strike which it had threatened. It is doubtful whether, with its lack of authority over the unions, it would have secured a response had it called for such a strike.

On July 12th, 1839, the petition for the Charter signed by one and a half million people was rejected by Parliament by 235 votes to 46. The Convention was unable to reply. The physical force section tried to organize insurrectionary actions but were unable to do anything commensurable with the needs of the situation. The biggest action was that of the insurgents led by John Frost who set out to secure a forcible release of the Chartist, Henry Vincent, from Newport gaol. A thousand men set out with Frost at their head. They were met by the military. Ten were killed, fifty wounded, and the movement crushed.

Within four months four hundred and fifty men were arrested. O'Connor, O'Brien and Frost were charged with high treason. Thus ended the first phase of Chartism.

The second phase of Chartism began in July, 1840, with the formation of the National Chartist Association. This was a *well organized Workers' Party*, the first definite party organization in the history of the British working class. It comprised four hundred local organizations and forty thousand members. It issued membership cards, held congresses and had its regularly established executive committee. It defied the law concerning national organization. It introduced a new petition adding economic and social demands entirely absent from the first Charter petition. It protested against the terrible poverty, the low wages, the murderous Poor Law, the high taxes, the long hours of labour and abuses of the factory legislation. It denounced the class legislation directed against the workers.

Three hundred and thirty-one thousand signatures were

obtained for the petition during a period when the capitalist class was seeking to divert the attention of the workers by a powerful agitation for the repeal of the Corn Laws.

In 1842 the Chartist struggle was intensified by trade union strikes. The unions had up to this time ignored the Chartist Movement.

The workers declared themselves in favour of a general strike, popularly known in the ranks of Chartism as the 'sacred month'. The strike movement spread throughout the industrial areas. Again the country was in a condition verging on civil war. And again the Government won. Fifteen hundred arrests were made. The Chartist Association suffered severely. Membership dropped to three or four thousand. It finally perished. The trade unions turned to limited economic action.

The end of this second period of Chartism coincided with another period of trade recovery lasting from 1843 to 1846. It was in this period that the Co-operative Movement secured a footing and the middle class elements within the Chartist Movement associated with land schemes raised the cry of 'back to the land'. O'Connor, editor and publisher of the *Northern Star*, the central organ of Chartism, was the principal spokesman on this question. He was really the voice of the smallholder. Marx describes him as – 'by nature a conservative' and 'all his ideas are thoroughly patriarchal and bourgeois'.

The third and final phase of Chartism followed the commercial crisis which began in 1847. It was inspired and influenced by the revolution of February, 1848, in France. The Irish Famine also had its effect upon the movement owing to the large influx of Irish workers and the horrible indifference of the ruling classes to the sufferings of the Irish workers and peasants. The Chartist Movement throughout its history maintained a keen interest in and contact with international events and movements. The *Poor Man's Guardian* and the *Northern Star*, the great newspapers of Chartism, with big circulations, provide abundant evidence in their pages of great interest in international affairs. The cause of Ireland was kept constantly before the masses. Great demonstrations of sympathy with the Polish people in their struggle against Czarism were frequently organized. Harney and Jones, two of the best leaders of Chartism, were members of an international organization known as the Fraternal Democrats, and later, members of the First International.

Hence it is no matter of surprise that the continental revolutions of 1848 found a warm response in the ranks of British Chartism. Many messages of congratulation were sent from the British workers to the French Revolutionaries.

Another Chartist Convention was organized for April 3rd, 1848. 1,975,000 signatures were collected in support of another petition. It was agreed that if this petition was rejected a National Convention would be convened and remain in session until the Charter demands became the law of the land.

On April 10th a tremendous meeting was to be organized on Kennington Green which was to march to Parliament in support of the Chartist petition. The Government prepared as never before. London was turned into an armed camp. But only thirty to forty thousand people turned up to the demonstration, due to the effect of intimidation, wavering leadership and bad organization. It was a complete failure. The petition for which it had been boasted not less than five million signatures had been secured was wholly discredited when later it was discovered that half of them were faked signatures. This was the end of the Chartist Movement.

From this moment the working class were in retreat from the revolutionary path. Chartism did not revive. The end of Chartism in 1848 marks the end of an epoch in the history of international capitalism and the working-class movement. It was the epoch of the rise and triumph of industrial capitalism, of the emergence of the proletariat as a class undertaking tasks and aspiring to a goal it could reach *only when capitalism had completed its own revolutionary role and become an impediment to the progressive development of society*.

The reasons for the defeat of Chartism therefore lay in the very nature of the historic position of capitalism at this time.

Circumstances over which they had no control now diverted the working class from rapidly advancing towards further revolutionary struggles. Britain was placed in an unique situation. British capitalism had achieved an undisputed world-leadership with all her potential rivals well behind her. New gold discoveries in Australia and California gave a great impetus to emigration. Expanding markets opened up before British capitalism everywhere. The great epoch of capitalist expansion had begun.

It was on the basis of this situation that the Corn Laws were repealed in 1846; that real wages began to rise; that the Ten Hour Bill was passed; that factory legislation was introduced. The concessions to the workers were the by-products of their revolutionary struggles, but by-products that were granted because of the changed situation.

A subject class cannot make a revolution and overthrow

the class above it when that class is still advancing economically and politically and has scope to postpone the final revolutionary attack by means of large-scale concessions which result in a higher standard of life for the class below it. Classes do not make revolutions in such circumstances. A revolution is a tremendous social event. Its dynamic forces are millions upon millions of people who feel and know that the making of a fundamental change in society is a matter of life or death. Revolution is the outcome when a system can no longer develop the forces of production upon which progressive economic and social development depends. This is why the English revolution of 1688 and the French Revolution of 1789 settled accounts with Feudalism and why it was not possible for the working class of the eighteenth and nineteenth centuries to settle accounts with capitalism – and why it will settle accounts with it in the twentieth century.

But there was still another contributory cause to the failure of Chartism to advance further. Up to the close of the Chartist Movement the working class were led by leaders who had not arrived at scientific socialism. All their teachings, all their aspirations reflected the utopian aspirations of idealist philosophers and poets, inspired principally by the doctrines associated with the bourgeois revolutions, especially the French Revolution. They talked of 'natural law' and the 'rights of man'. They exposed the wrongs of a class-ridden society They advocated a society free from class rule. They conjured visions of a classless society. They thought they could have private property and control it. They did not distinguish between economic and political power. But they did not understand the laws of social development.

Without such knowledge the leaders of the working class could not understand how and when the victory could be achieved.

The whole period, however, in which the industrial revolution had taken place in England was also a period of great development of the capitalist revolutions in France and Germany History was therefore rich with the materials for scientific analysis, for drawing scientific conclusions. Such analysis was made. Such scientific conclusions were drawn. The advance of capitalism revolutionizes the productive process at every step and inevitably brings with it an advance of science in general and the growth of the scientific method in all departments of human thought. It was out of these developments with their repercussions in philosophy and political economy that the intelligentsia of capitalism provided the men who transformed socialism from a utopian dream to a scientific doctrine. The man who, more than any other, was responsible for this transformation was Karl Marx. The first document propounding scientific socialism was the 'Communist Manifesto', written in 1847 and first published in 1848. The publisher of the English edition was Harney, the Chartist.

The period of the initiation of the working class of this country as a revolutionary class ends, therefore, not on the note of fiasco but of certain victory. The mass movement retreats on the tide of circumstance but scientific socialism arrives. So important is this fact that we will consider its significance further in another chapter.

CHAPTER II

THE SIGNIFICANCE OF THE COMMUNIST MANIFESTO

It is a significant reflection on the insularity of most of the British Labour historians that they have always detached the 'Communist Manifesto' from the British working-class movement. It is treated not as an international document which belongs to the working class of each country, but as a foreign document politely labelled 'international'. Yet it is impossible to read this pronouncement without recognizing that of all countries which provided the material upon which its analysis was made, none was so rich, none so far advanced as Britain itself, and none more deeply considered

In the writer's opinion no history of the British, German, and French labour movements in particular, is correctly written if it does not mark off the publication of the 'Communist Manifesto' as an event of the utmost importance in the development of the movement of that country. It is not enough to designate it as an 'international event' and leave it at that. Precisely because of its international character and significance it cannot be separated from the life of the respective national labour movements, especially of the period which gave rise to it.

It may be argued that few people took notice of its publication at the time and that it did not immediately become the accepted guide to the actions of the working-class movement. That it was not so accepted, of course, is quite true. One may ask what new scientific teaching has ever received a spontaneous welcome?

Max Beer in his *History of British Socialism*, p. 102, shows that prior to Marx the common basis of all the writers associated with the workers' movement was as follows:

> 'Common possession was natural and therefore just and equitable; Labour was the only title to property or wealth; Nature, including human nature, was governed by inherent, divine, and rational laws.
> 'Hence it followed:—
> 'That private property was unnatural and pernicious, and ought to be abolished; That all deductions from the produce of labour, in the shape of rent, profit, and interest, by non-labourers, constituted a violation of natural law; That all reform must be directed towards the restoration of, or be in harmony with, natural law.'[1]

On the basis of their analysis of capitalism most bitter criticisms were made of the existing social order, but it must be obvious that, so long as 'natural right' and 'injustice' were the guiding ideas they could only lead, on the one hand to dreams of a new social order, either through social upheaval or moral persuasion, or on the other hand to the extraction from the immediate situation of such reforms as could be secured through bargaining or restricted struggles.

The tactical experiments that were actually made in this period prove conclusively that they were not arrived at on the grounds of a larger strategy based upon a con-

[1] The principal exponents of the theories were – Spence, Ogilvie, Paine (agrarian reformers),– the quondam communists Godwin, Coleridge, Southey, and the London Corresponding Society, who took their inspiration from the French Revolution – Hall, Owen, Thompson, Ravenstone, Dray, Hodgskin the communist and anti-capitalist critics.

The economists of the period were Patrick Colquhoun, Smith, Ricardo, Thompson and Ravenstone. For full exposition of their views see Max Beer's *History of British Socialism*, p. 102.

sideration of the relation of social forces and their historical development, but rather as flaming revolts against injustice, or short cuts to revolution. Owen spoke of the change coming 'like a thief in the night'. Morrison and Smith, the class war syndicalists, were fascinated with the idea of Benbow – 'There will not be insurrection; it will simply be passive resistance. The men may remain at leisure; there is, and can be, no law to compel them to work against their will . . . and what happens as a consequence? Bills are dishonoured, the Gazette teems with bankruptcies, capital is destroyed, the revenue fails, the system of government falls into confusion, and every link in the chain which binds society together is broken in a moment by this inert conspiracy of the poor against the rich.'

They had yet to learn that a ruling class is not so easily disposed of and that its resistance will be more than passive resistance. A general strike may be a demonstration limited to short duration. It may be a form of mass pressure on a government. It may be the precursor of insurrection. In every case it is a political challenge to the State. No State could regard the stoppage of the productive machinery of society otherwise than as a challenge to its existence. It will retreat, compromise or take issue with it, according to its considered power to defeat the strike. To enter into a general strike without appreciating these facts and all they imply, and to work out a strategy and tactics accordingly, is to ask for defeat.

Later, it is true, the physical force Chartists went farther than Morrison and Smith and Benbow, and declared for the use of weapons and the settling of accounts by force of arms.

At the other extreme were the trade unionists and co-operators, who in increasing numbers felt the futility of mass assaults on the system which were repeatedly defeated. These turned their attention towards more limited objectives, such as collective bargaining and the building of Consumers Co-operative societies, not because they had become acquainted with a new theory of social development, but because they felt they must adapt themselves to the existing system. Mr. and Mrs. Webb in their *History of Trades Unionism* regard the leaders of this phase of the movement very sympathetically, as representatives of 'that spirit of cautious if somewhat limited statesmanship which characterized the trade union leaders of the next thirty years' and save all their biting comments for the revolutionaries.

Actually, however, they have no more claim to be regarded as 'the brains' of the movement than the revolutionaries who wished to leap to the new social order. Their teachings concerning the situation obtaining in their day and generation proved equally fallacious in their own practice. Nothing demonstrated this more effectively than the fate of the 'National Association of United Trades' formed in 1845. This organization was led by those who 'were deeply impressed with the importance of, and beneficial tendency arising from, a good understanding between the employer and the employed; *seeing that their interests are mutual*, and that neither can injure the other without the wrong perpetrated recoiling upon the party who inflicts it, etc.'

Despite this repudiation of the class war the 'National Association' went the way of the Grand National Consolidated Union of the earlier period, and for exactly the same reasons. The class war was so fierce and the calls upon the central funds of the organization so numerous, owing to the many local strikes and lock-outs, that the union finally perished. It perished of the class war it repudiated. The leaders did not understand the period any more than the revolutionaries had understood it. There is no justification, therefore, for regarding these leaders as the men of virtue and the revolutionaries as the stupid wild men. Both alike represent the immaturity of the working-class movement and the primitive stage of the development of socialist theory.

The appearance of the 'Communist Manifesto' at the end of this period of revolutionary mass activity was too late to influence the Chartist Movement. Nevertheless it is the crowning gift of this epoch to the future generations.

That Marx and Engels had studied the situation in England is unquestioned. Engels, who first came to England in 1842, was a contributor to the *Northern Star*, the organ of the Chartists. Both Marx and Engels became close friends of the Chartist leaders Jones and Harney. Hence the material contact of the authors of the 'Communist Manifesto' with the British working-class movement is as clearly manifest as the inner content of the document reveals the understanding of the industrial revolution in England.

'The basic thought underlying the Manifesto,' says Engels in his preface to the German edition of 1883, is as follows:

> 'the method of production, and the organization of social life inevitably arising therefrom, constitute in every historical epoch the foundation upon which is built the political and intellectual history of that epoch; consequently (ever since the disappearance of

communal ownership of land) the whole of man's history has been the history of class struggles, incessant warfare between exploited and exploiter, between oppressed classes and ruling classes at various stages in the evolution of society; the struggle has now reached a stage of development when the exploited and oppressed class (the proletariat) cannot free itself from the dominion of the exploiting and ruling class (the bourgeoisie) without at one and the same time and for ever ridding society of exploitation, oppression and class struggles.'

With this guiding thought running through the Manifesto, Marx analyses the origin and development of capitalism, the nature of its crises, the development of the forces which will destroy it and outlines a programme for the first socialist government.

The Manifesto explains that 'Our own age, the bourgeois age is distinguished by this – that it has simplified class antagonisms. More and more, society is splitting into two great hostile camps, into two great and directly contraposed classes; bourgeoisie and proletariat . . .' – 'The bourgeoisie cannot exist without revolutionizing the instruments of production; and consequently, the relations of production; and therefore the totality of social relations. . . . That which characterizes the bourgeois epoch in contradistinction to all others is a continuous transformation of production, a perpetual disturbance of social conditions, everlasting insecurity and movement. . .'

Marx vividly describes the crises of capitalism in words which read like a description of the world situation of to-day, 'Commercial crises,' he says, 'periodically lead to the destruction of a great part, not only of the finished products of industry, but also of the extant forces of production. During the crises a social epidemic breaks out, an epidemic that would have seemed absurdly paradoxical in all earlier phases of the world's history – an epidemic of over-production. Temporarily, society relapses into barbarism. It is as if a famine, or a universal, devastating war, had suddenly cut off the means of subsistence. Industry and commerce have to all seeming, been utterly destroyed. Why is this? Because society has too much civilization, too much industry, too much commerce. The productive forces at the disposal of the community no longer serve to foster bourgeois property relations . . .

'The bourgeois system is no longer able to cope with the abundance of the wealth it creates. How does the bourgeoisie overcome these crises? On the one hand by the compulsory annihilation of a quantity of the productive forces; on the other hand by the conquest of new markets and the more thorough exploitation of old ones. With what results? The results are that the way is paved for more widespread and more disastrous crises and that the capacity for averting such crises is lessened. . . .'

Of the proletariat the Manifesto says, it 'passes through various stages of evolution, but the struggle against the bourgeoisie dates from its birth . . . As industry develops, the proletariat does not merely increase in numbers; it is compacted into larger masses; its strength grows; it is more aware of its strength . . . Unity is furthered by the improvement in the means of communication which are effected by large scale industry and brings the workers of different localities into closer contact . . . The organization of the proletarians to form a class and therewith to form a political party is perpetually becoming disintegrated by competition amongst the workers themselves.

Yet it is incessantly reformed, becoming stronger, firmer, mightier . . . The chief requisite for capital is wage labour. Now, wage labour depends exclusively upon competition among the workers. The progress of industry, which the bourgeoisie involuntarily and passively promotes, substitutes for the isolation of the workers by mutual competition, their revolutionary unification by association. . . . Before all, therefore the bourgeoisie produces its own grave diggers. Its downfall and the victory of the proletariat are equally inevitable.'

Most important are the observations on the relation of the communists to the general body of the working class. It is quite obvious from this manifesto that Marx visualized the evolution of a working-class party on the broadest possible basis. The duty of the communists was to advocate the interests of the movement as a whole against the exploiters of the working class, in terms of the class struggle. The Manifesto says: '*Communists do not form a separate party conflicting with other working class parties.* They have no interests apart from those of the working class as a whole. They do not put forward any sectarian principles with which they wish to mould the proletarian movement . . . in actual practice communists form the most resolute and persistently progressive section of the working-class parties of all lands; whilst as far as theory is concerned, being in advance of the general mass of the proletariat, they have come to understand the determinants of the proletarian movement, and how to foresee its course and its general results. . . .'

It is asserted by some communists (see *From Chartism to Labourism*, by Th. Rothstein) that this was a special concession to the British Chartists. Why so important a principle should be imposed upon the whole International working-class movement without explanation by the authors of the document we are not told. Had Marx and Engels thought of making 'a concession to the Chartists' in a theoretical document they would have made it in a footnote and not in the main text of the document.

This principle conflicts with the present relation of communists to the labour movement. Why there is this divergence it will be necessary to discuss later. Sufficient at this stage to observe the clear formulation of the line of advance to be taken by the working class, the recognition of the urgent need of a political party of the working class and the relationship of the advance guard to such a party.

For the first time also, the Manifesto laid the foundations of a programme for a working-class government. At this time it must be noticed that Marx had not worked out the precise form of this government which he defined as 'the proletariat organized as a ruling class'. The programme, however, is far in advance of anything that had yet appeared. He says:

'In most advanced countries they will, generally speaking, take the following forms:—

1. Expropriation of landed property, and the use of land rents to defray State expenditure.
2. A vigorously graduated income tax.
3. Abolition of all right of inheritance.
4. Confiscation of the property of all emigrés and rebels.
5. Centralization of credit in the hands of the State, by means of a national bank with state capital and an exclusive monopoly.
6. Centralization of the means of transport in the hands of the state.

> 7. Increase of national factories and means of production, cultivation of uncultivated land, and improvement of cultivated land in accordance with the general plan.
> 8. Universal and equal obligation to work; organization of industrial armies, especially for agriculture.
> 9. Agriculture and urban industries to work hand in hand, in such a way as, by degrees to obliterate the distinction between town and country.
> 10. Public and free education of all children. Abolition of all factory work for children in its present form. Education and material production to be combined. . . .'

Whether the Manifesto be compared with the theories of Morrison and Smith, of Owen or of the new sturdy trade union leaders, comparison ends in contrast. The utopians are brought down to earth and compelled to stand on their feet instead of their heads. Once the principles of the new Marxian science of society are grasped, the short-sighted local tradc unionist and co-operator is able to understand his own origins and to see what the next step must be. These teachings were not readily assimilated by the masses for the reasons which led to the decline of the revolutionary movement of Chartism.

This failure had far reaching consequences. It meant that in the absence of a revolutionary party inspired with scientific socialism, co-ordinating and directing the unions and the co-operatives, the workers' clubs and newspapers, the workers were subject to their immediate local influences. Reacting strongly against the failures of the revolutionary movement it was the most natural thing in the word that they flocked to the banner of 'No Politics' held aloft by liberal capitalism growing fat with prosperity.

Nevertheless, the inexorable operation of the class antagonisms of capitalist society led the workers into building their own class organizations with which the fight for their independent class aims would inevitably be renewed.

CHAPTER III

THE HEYDAY OF REFORMISM

THE years from 1850 to 1900 are an epoch in which British industrial capitalism expanded in all directions and was finally transformed into 'monopoly capitalism', i.e. imperialism. It was a period of incessant struggle between the workers and the capitalists, but all the struggles had a definitely limited objective – that of a share in the profits of capitalism.

Although the working class throughout this period had no political party and the strikes were limited in their scope and size, there was a great growth of working-class organization, a centralization of forces locally, nationally and internationally, and the signs of a coming break with capitalist liberalism by the working class.

From 1850 to 1870 British capitalism had an undisputed monopoly of the world market, but it was still in the period of 'free competition'. Its monopoly consisted in the fact that it had become the workshop of the world and was years ahead of its potential rivals in the development of its industries. It carried forward all the gains of the industrial revolution to their logical conclusion.

In 1834 there were 8,000,000 spindles at work. In 1868 England possessed 30,478,728 spindles. Between the years 1834 and 1868 the number of workers employed in the mills increased from 220,000 to 396,852. In the same period the number of power looms increased from 110,000 to 379,000. The output of iron reached 3,218,000 tons in 1855. In the same year 246,613 workers were employed in the mines and produced 61,000,000 tons of coal. There were 12,789 miles of railway in the United Kingdom in 1864 and 94,665 sailors engaged in the merchant service in 1861.[1]

Exports rose in the twenty years 1846 to 1866 from £58,842,377 to £188,917,563. Incomes coming under income tax rose from £307,068,878 in 1856 to £385,530,020 in 1865.

Industry became ever more concentrated. Marx draws attention to the fact that the number of factories in the United Kingdom in 1861 was 2,887, but in 1868 the number had decreased to 2,549 whilst production had increased. He cites as an example of the process going on the evidence of Mr. Nasmyth, an employer giving evidence before the Government commission on trade unionism appointed after the long strikes of the engineers in 1851. He stated that 'Thanks to these new mechanical combinations I have reduced the number of grown-up men from 1500 to 750. The result was a considerable increase in my profits."[1]

Everywhere throughout the country Joint Stock Companies were formed and became a feature of the economic system of the period. Thus the pace was set for the growth of trusts and monopolies.

The year 1870 marked the actual end of Britain's 'free competition' monopoly of the world market. Modern capitalism had by this time got into its stride in Germany, France and America. In this year Germany dispossessed France of Alsace-Lorraine with its iron ore deposits. The United States of America reaches the output level of Britain's iron and steel production. The 'boom' in

[1] A most complete analysis of this period is made by Marx in vol. i of *Capital*, chapters xv and xvi.

[2] *Capital*, vol. i, p. 476.

colonial annexation by the chief European states began.

According to Sir R. Giffen (quoted by J. A. Hobson in *Imperialism*), between the years 1870 and 1898 Britain added to its domains 4,784,000 square miles of territory with an estimated population of 88,000,000. France acquired in the same period 37,000,000 square miles with a population of 36,000,000. Germany acquired 1,000,000 square miles with a population of 14,700,000 inhabitants. The other powers were busy, too, in the same direction, until the whole world was completely parcelled out between them, the big powers of course swallowing up the biggest shares. There were then no new lands to conquer. Any new divisions would have o be re-division of the spoils.[1]

This expansion increased the opportunities for the export of capital. Between 1862 and 1914 the yearly export of capital rose from £3.6 millions to £100 millions. The growing importance of the banks is seen at a glance in the fact that by 1910 Britain had 72 colonial banks with not less than 5,449 branches. France had twenty banks with 136 branches.[2] By 1899 British capitalism derived £100,000,000 revenue from capital invested abroad as compared with £18,000,000 obtained from its import and export trade. Thus Britain's position as the 'workshop of the world' was passing away.[3] In its

[1] See Lenin's *Imperialism*, chapter vi. [2] Ibid., pp. 66–67.

[3] TRADE RETURNS IN THE YEAR 1887. (IMPORTS)

	Total Imports	*From England*	*From other Countries*
	£	£	£
Russia	39,321,000	5,868,849	33,462,151
Germany	230,100,000	27,316,544	202,783,456
Belgium	116,266,000	13,140,582	103,125,418
France	197,708,000	20,495,730	177,212,270
Holland	94,457,000	15,037,525	79,419,475
U.S.A.	144,233,000	40,240,150	103,992,850

[*See next page*]

stead international capitalism took the form of a struggle between monopolies headed by the finance capitalists.

The effect of these developments upon the working class of this period were enormous. According to Professor Bowley the wages of the cotton workers rose thirty per cent between 1855 and 1874. The wages of the Lancashire miners rose from three shillings and eightpence per day to four shillings and fourpence per day between 1851 and 1880. The wages of woollen workers rose fifteen per cent between 1857 and 1870. These were but symptomatic of the general tendency of the period. It is further estimated that between 1870 and the end of the century the tendency was still upwards, averaging seventeen per cent in the various industries.

But the most important feature of these times is the change in the price level. Th. Rothstein, who analyses in some detail the price and wage tendencies of this period in his book *From Chartism to Labourism*, estimates that between 1877 and 1895 the fall in prices meant a fifty per cent decrease in the cost of living.

This is why Engels was able to write in 1892 in his preface to a new edition of *The Condition of the Working Class in England in 1844:*

TRADE RETURNS IN THE YEAR 1887. (EXPORTS)

	Total Exports £	To England £	To other Countries £
Russia	62,295,000	9,683,388	52,611,613
Germany	231,235,000	24,563,536	206,671,464
Belgium	108,612,000	14,732,663	93,879,337
France	169,528,000	38,855,296	130,672,704
Holland	94,457,000	25,327,277	57,299,723
U.S.A.	149,204,000	83,049,074	66,154,926

– cf., *Commonweal*, April 5th, 1888.

> 'The truth is this: during the period of England's industrial monopoly the English working class have, to a certain extent, shared in the benefits of the monopoly. These benefits were very unequally parcelled out amongst them; the privileged minority pocketed most, but even the great mass had, at least, a temporary share now and then. And that is the reason why, since the dying out of Owenism, there has been no socialism in England.'

At the same time it must not be assumed that this was a period in which there were no struggles or that poverty had been eliminated or even that the workers were on a uniformly low level which had been uniformly raised. There was always a great army of unemployed workers and in no year between 1859 and 1909 were there less than 800,000 workers forced to apply for parish relief. Besides this glaring evidence of mass poverty it is important to remember that the net balance of emigration over immigration between the year 1876 and 1909 is not less than 4,147,007. These two sets of facts tell us plainly of the severity of the position of the working class. It was a period marked by recurring crises, many strikes and unemployed protest movements.

But the strikes were not revolutionary. They aimed at securing collective bargains between the workers and the employers. The strikes were conducted, especially in the early part of this period, mainly by the skilled workers. They were led by men who hated strikes, and openly advocated class collaboration. That invaluable mine of information, the Webbs's *History of Trade Unionism* provides abundant evidence of how hateful strikes and lock-outs were to them. 'The Stonemasons' Central Committee repeatedly cautioned their members against the dangerous practice of striking . . . "Keep from it", they urge "as you would from a ferocious animal that you know would destroy you. . . ."' The Flint Glass Makers' magazine declared, 'strikes have been the bane of trades unions'. The Moulders vested the entire authority as to strike action in their executive in order to counter all tendencies for their local organizations to initiate strikes.

It was this setting of the face of trade unionism against strikes that led to their attempt to control the distribution of labour in industry. The trade union leaders argued that wages depended on supply and demand and accordingly strengthened their attitude towards apprenticeship with a view to restricting the number of apprentices and to the encouragement of emigration. A number of unions went so far as to create a fund from which to aid unemployed members to emigrate.

The whole period is full of such attempts to escape the class war. They did not aspire to become the ruling class. They repudiated the idea of unified class organization. Each union wanted to be on its own and on good terms with the employers. Their highest aspiration for the workers was for them to be respectable citizens of capitalist society. Politics they wanted to leave to liberal gentlemen. All of which was as utopian as the dreams of Owen and the early revolutionaries.

They could not escape the class war. They were compelled by the force of circumstances to wage it. Capitalist competition forced the workers into conflict with the employers for their daily bread despite their desire to avoid the conflict. The centralization of their organizations and the drawing together of all workers' organizations, which was so emphatically rejected as revolutionary, was forced upon them by daily experience. The independent class politics of Chartism which they had abandoned for liberalism steadily reappeared out of the struggles against new anti-trade union laws.

The whole of this period of British working-class history has been written down as non-revolutionary, and critics have either regarded it as a period in which the working class were grossly betrayed or have welcomed the 'statesmanship' of the leaders and the correctness of their vision. It was certainly the heyday of opportunism enriching itself on the fatty accretions of expanding capitalism and imperialism.

It was inevitable, therefore, that the development of the working class as an independent class with its own distinctly revolutionary aims, had to proceed in the face of opportunism, political backwardness and ideological subservience to capitalism. But the most important fact to observe is that this development *did* proceed, its aims *did* emerge. It is by this fact that Marxism, i.e. scientific socialism, is abundantly justified.

Out of the sympathetic strike actions of the trade unions grew more permanent class organizations, destined to figure prominently in great class actions of the workers on a scale which was certainly not anticipated at their inception. First of these organizations were the Trades Councils, first formed in Sheffield, Glasgow, and Edinburgh in 1860. In these trades councils gathered delegates from the various trades unions in the locality. They elected an executive committee representative of all the affiliated trade unions. Often they grew directly out of strike committees. They rapidly spread to all the most important industrial centres. It is only necessary here to refer to their role as mobilizers of the working class in 1917 for the Congress of Workers' Councils supporting the Russian Revolution, their part in the Councils of Action in the threatened General Strike of 1920 to stop the war of intervention against Russia, and their part in the General Strike of 1926, to recognize that whatever the intentions of the founders of trades councils, they builded better than they knew.

Thus the law of the concentration and consolidation of working class forces, indicated by Marx in the 'Communist Manifesto', was operating relentlessly as a result of the development of the social methods of production and the operation of class antagonisms. This took place in spite of the workers' organizations being in the hands of leaders who repudiated the theory which corresponded to the facts.

The same process forced the unions to concentrate on a national scale The amalgamation of numerous organizations was a feature of the period. By the end of the century there were two million workers enrolled in the ranks of the trade unions. In 1868 there was the first national gathering of the unions since the collapse of the 'National Association of United Trades' in the first half of the century. The Trades Union Congress was thus established, not as an act of class war but to aid the struggle of the unions to become a recognized part of capitalism. They had no idea then that some day the Trade Union Congress would be the vehicle for launching a general strike.

Four years prior to the establishment of the Trades Union Congress a most important step was taken in the unification of the ranks of the workers in the formation of the 'International Working-men's Association', known historically as the First International. Its most important predecessor was the international organization of Fraternal Democrats already referred to, as led by the Chartists, Ernest Jones and Harney. This latter organization was broken up after the defeat of the revolutionary movements in Europe in 1848 and the defeat of Chartism in this country.

The First International was formed in September, 1864. The committee which established it was composed of English and French workers and the German and Italian emigrants living in London. London was its base throughout its history. Its political composition was a mixture of Owenites, Trade Unionists, Chartists, followers of Proudhon and Blanqui of France, German Communists, Polish and Italian Nationalists. Later it drew in the Russian Bakunin and his anarchist followers, a not unimportant factor in shortening the life of the International.

Karl Marx was the outstanding figure of the International. The programme and statutes of this organization were drafted by him. The statutes of the International set forth the following:

> 'The emancipation of the working class must be the work of the working classes themelves . . . Considering: That the economical subjection of the men of labour to the monopolizer of the means of labour, that is, the sources of life, lies at the bottom of servitude in all its forms, of all social misery, mental degradation and political dependence;
>
> 'That the economical emancipation of the working classes is therefore the great end to which every political movement ought to be subordinate as a means;

> 'That all efforts aiming at that great end have hitherto failed from the want of solidarity between the manifold divisions of labour in each country, and from the absence of a fraternal bond of union between the working classes of different countries;
>
> 'That the emancipation of labour is neither a local, nor a national, but a social problem, embracing all countries in which modern society exists, and depending for its solution on the concurrence, practical and theoretical, of the most advanced countries.'

The organization of the International was based upon national sections managed by a National Federation Council under the ideological guidance of the General Council of the International. The history of its proceedings gives a classic example of what Marx conceived the role of a communist to be in an organization composed of diverse elements yet founded upon the broad class foundations of the workers.

The Communist League which had issued the 'Manifesto of the Communist Party' was not a party of action but of propaganda. The International was an organization for action and throughout its history Marx continuously waged a fight for the application of the principles of scientific socialism whilst striving to hold together the most contradictory elements.

The English trade unions were the basis of the International, though ideologically the most backward. The English Chartists, Jones and Harney, were the most advanced and revolutionary of the English representatives. The trade unionists were there only for definite trade union ends. The British workers connected with these unions had a higher standard of life than the continental workers and were deeply concerned with the importation of continental workers during strikes.

The interest in international action was not one-sided. International solidarity during strikes became a reality and the British trade unions contributed liberally, both financially and by sympathetic mass action, in support of continental disputes. They participated, too, in many international political demonstrations, but the subservience of the trade union leaders to 'liberalism' was most marked. Leaders such as Odgers, Howell, Osborne, and Applegarth had no sympathy for socialism of any kind, scientific or utopian.

Marx, however, looked upon the International as the beginning of an international workers' party, with communist tendencies. The preamble of the International visualized the coming of an international revolution starting in the most advanced countries. History has proved such an estimate to be entirely wrong though it was perfectly natural that the International should arise in those countries first, because the growth of the proletariat is dependent upon the growth of capitalism. Without the latter there is no proletariat, but the question of where and when the proletariat overcomes the bourgeoisie after capitalism has become an international phenomenon, is an entirely different one. This declaration in the preamble led to the widespread acceptance of the theory that the proletarian revolution would take place first in the most advanced countries, a point of view which was completely disproved by the Russian Revolution in 1917.

The aim of the socialists to draw the workers into politics and to develop the International as an International Workers' Party was frustrated by two events –

the internal disputes with the anarchists and the defeat of the Paris Commune.

The Bakunists (Anarchists) were against the formation of independent working class parties. They opposed political action altogether. Nothing less than an immediate social revolution involving the destruction of the State and dispensing with all forms of government would content them. Marx, on the other hand, when it became clear that the early transformation of the International into a party was not possible, stood for the organization of the workers into separate national political parties. These parties were to work constantly in the interests of the workers, aiming at the democratization of society and the conquest of power by the proletariat.

The English trade union leaders lagged behind the Marxists on the most elementary questions, such as the formation of a workers' party. After the defeat of the Paris Commune all the contending factions of the International disputed on this, the greatest experience of the proletarian movement.

Up to the time of the Commune the principal activities of the International were economic. This accounts for the big part that the British trade unions played in the history of the International prior to this event. The suppression of the Commune, however, forced the question of the creation of independent working-class parties into the foreground. This issue conflicted with the point of view of the Bakunists, the followers of Proudhon and a section of the British trade unionists. In the conference discussion which followed in September, 1871, the Marxists won. But the dispute broke the International.

The Conference declared that 'the International was faced with unbridled reaction which paralysed every effort of the workers to achieve their emancipation and which intended to maintain by force the distinction between the classes and the consequent dominance of the possessing classes. Against the collective power of the possessing classes the proletariat could only act as a class by forming itself into an independent political party standing in opposition to the old parties formed by the possessing classes. . . .'[1]

The First International was finally liquidated in 1874. The final Convention held in Philadelphia published a declaration which contains the following:

> ' "The International is dead!" the bourgeoisie of all countries will exclaim, and with ridicule and joy it will point to the proceedings of this convention as documentary proof of the defeat of the labour movement of the whole world. Let us not be influenced by the cry of our enemies! We have abandoned the organization of the International for reasons arising from the present political situation of Europe, but as a compensation for it we see the principles of the organization recognized and defended by the progressive working men of the entire civilized world. Let us give our fellow-workers in Europe a little time to strengthen their national affairs, and they will surely soon be in a position to remove the barriers between themselves and the working men of other parts of the world. . . .'

Thus the working-class movement in each country was thrown back on its own resources. But the First International had succeeded in spreading the idea of international working-class solidarity amongst the workers, especially the trade unionists of Britain who in several

[1] *History of First International*, by Stekloff, p. 251.

industries were the first again to take the initiative in the building of international federations of the unions.

Although the British leaders had played a conservative part in the politics of the International the latter had done much to spread revolutionary ideas amongst the workers of this country. A number of the British leaders, despite their general conservatism, had also done considerable work in the propagation of the idea of an independent workers' political party. This propaganda was conducted through the British section of the International, reinforced by several other organizations propagating independent labour representation in Parliament, e.g. The London Working-men's Union (1866-68), the Labour Representation League (1869-80) But the most decisive influence finally came through the Trades Councils and was based upon the struggles of the unions against various Acts of Parliament.

A group of trade union leaders known as the Junta, which included Applegarth of the Carpenters' Union and William Allen of the Engineers, dominated the London Trades Council. Through this body they made great efforts to interest the unions in politics Alexander MacDonald and Campbell of the Miners assisted them considerably. It was the two latter who were reponsible for the agitation through all the trades councils which secured the amendment of the law relating to Masters and Servants in 1867. The law at that time limited the masters to fines for offences but penalized the workers by terms of imprisonment. The amendment of this law was a big step forward for the workers, liberating them from considerable oppression and giving them greater confidence in their own organizations, although the change was carried through under the banner of liberalism.

The next struggle concerned the law relating to Trade Unions, especially the Criminal Law Amendment Act. The Government had conceded the existence of the trade unions as legal trade societies and then stretched the Criminal Law to fetter their activities. It was the agitation on this question which led the miners, ironworkers and others to vote money in support of parliamentary candidates. At the elections of 1874 thirteen working-men candidates went to the poll. All of them were liberals. Two miners' leaders, MacDonald and Burt, were elected. Immediately afterwards Disraeli passed a new Trades Union Bill which satisfied the organized workers and once more there was a lull in the development of independent labour politics. This illustrates the tortuous way in which the class antagonisms have forced their way through the class collaboration ideology which dominated the working-class movement, and compelled the working class to advance to new positions of independence.

The next important advance came in the footsteps of the commercial crisis of 1878-79 and 1886-87. In these years began the definite formation of new political parties. The first of these was the Social Democratic Party formed in 1881 by H. M. Hyndman and a few intellectuals and workers. In 1883 it changed its name and became known as the Social Democratic Federation. It included in its ranks such well-known leaders as Tom Mann, John Burns, William Morris, Belfort Bax, Jack Williams and Harry Quelch. Although it announced itself as a Marxist organization, a comparison of its programme with that outlined by Marx in the 'Communist Manifesto', reveals the S.D.F. lagging behind the Manifesto in its conception of a programme for the working class. Its programme was only a little in advance of the demands of the Chartists.

It stood for 'Universal Suffrage', 'Triennial Parliaments', 'Equal Electoral Divisions', 'Payment of members', 'Corruption and Bribery at elections to be punishable as criminal offences', 'Abolition of the House of Lords', 'Home Rule for Ireland', 'Self-Government for the Colonies and Dependencies', 'Nationalization of the Land'.

Such a programme could not be considered as a programme of a class come to power or aiming at power. It was essentially reformist. In putting these forward it was at a disadvantage in that the language of the Social Democrats was much more revolutionary in temper than the demands warranted. Their speeches were based more upon the declared object of the Federation which was announced as follows:

> 'The Object of the Social Democratic Federation is the establishment of a free society, based upon the principles of political equality, with equal social rights for all and complete emancipation of labour.'

This of course gave plenty of scope for revolutionary speeches based upon a contrast between the conditions of capitalism and the aims of socialism. But nowhere is there evidence of a clear formulation of how the S.D.F. conceived they were going to lead the working class to this goal. In fact it was the absence of collective clarity on this question that led to a series of splits in the Federation.

In 1884 it issued a manifesto to the trade unions which said that:

> 'the unions have forgotten how to fight and have made peace with capitalism. They made no reference to the

> class struggle that really existed and must go on between capital and labour. . . . The trade unions, unhappily, only thought of improving the position of the favoured few affiliated to their body and were blind to the miseries of the masses. . . . Private property in the means of production must cease and associated labour with equal distribution of its produce must take its place.'

There may have been, indeed there was, plenty of moral justification for the attack thus made on the unions, but there is a lack of historical sense revealed in the statement. There is plenty of revolutionary impatience but no indication as to how they were to achieve the revolutionary objective.

This manifesto led to the first split. It had antagonized the unions. Tom Mann, Ben Tillet, and John Burns left the Federation. They also criticized the unions but launched a campaign for the 'New Unionism', seeking to broaden the basis of the craft unions and beginning the task of organizing the unskilled workers. Tom Mann became President of the Dockers' Union formed out of the great Dock Strike of 1889. The Gasworkers and General Labourers' Union was organized by Burns, Mann, Tillet, and Will Thorne. The National Union of Agricultural Labourers rapidly increased its membership. But the craft unions remained craft unions and the new General Labour unions steadily modelled themselves upon the craft unions.

Then disagreement arose with others of the Federation concerning reformism and Parliamentarism. William Morris led a minority which formed the Socialist League. He argued that 'the socalists hoped to see society transformed into something fundamentally different from capitalism. This meant revolution. The object of parliamentary institutions, on the contrary, was the preservation of society in its present form by the amendment of its defects. Reforms were only the insurance schemes of capitalism against revolution'.

Morris received the support of the Anarchists who went with him into the Socialist League. He, however, was not an Anarchist and the differences between him and his new allies led in a few years to the winding up of the League. Morris later re-joined the S.D.F. But it did not become a mass party.

Early in the '80's also, the Fabian Society was formed by Sidney Webb and G. B. Shaw. Here began the organization of socialist 'gradualism' destined to play an exceedingly important part in the history of the Labour Movement. It criticized Marxism and propounded the theory of forming capitalism into socialism through the spread of socialist opinion penetrating all the institutions of capitalism. It pooh-poohed class war politics and the idea of revolution, and welcomed every municpial 'flag pole' as an advance to socialism. It had no intention of becoming a mass party. It was, and remained, a small party of intellectuals aiming at securing the leadership of the leaders of the labour organizations. It gathered together a number of able men and women skilled in research and exceedingly well-informed.

The coming of the Fabians represents the passing of reformism out of the hands of liberalism into the hands of the reformist socialist intellectuals. The liberals were never able to obscure their capitalist basis. The Fabians liberalized socialism. This was a more deadly way of poisoning the wells of working class independence and spreading paralysis in the ranks of the workers. Instead of an assault upon capitalism by the working class it propounded the conversion of the capitalists and the middle classes to socialism by permeation. 'We are all socialists now,' soon became a capitalist slogan. Fabian socialism was not a call to battle but to the middle class parlour. Yet it gave coherence to the labour leaders who were feeling the limitations of liberalism, who were against mass struggle by the workers and who had arrived at the stage when they recognized the need for the formation of a Labour Party.

The most important effort of this period towards the establishment of a working-class party was the formation of the Independent Labour Party at Bradford in 1893. There were 120 delegates present at the inaugural conference. Keir Hardie was the principal leader of this party. Its first secretary was Tom Mann. The programme of the I.L.P. was much the same as that of the Social Democratic Federation, although it disclaimed Marxism and revolution. Its propaganda was essentially reformist. Its attitude to the trade unions contrasted with that of the S.D.F. It was warmly sympathetic to them and appealed to them to transfer their independent economic action to politics. Although officially opposed to class war teaching it used typical class war arguments in support of its claim for an independent labour party. So also did Blatchford and his *Clarion* propagandists. Indeed Blatchford stated the case brilliantly in class war terms. He said:

> 'If an employer's interests are opposed to yours in business, what reason have you for supposing that his interests and yours are not opposed in politics? If you oppose a man as an employer, why do you vote for him as a member of Parliament? His calling himself a

Liberal or Tory does not alter the fact that he is an employer. To be a trade unionist and fight for your class during a strike, and to be a Tory or a Liberal and fight against your class at an election is folly . . . Do you elect your employers as officials of your trade unions? Do you send employers as delegates to your Trades Union Congress? You would laugh at the suggestion . . .'

Thus the line taken by Marx and Engels became popular amongst all socialist groups. However confused and conflicting they may have been on a variety of questions, on the need for a Labour Party all were agreed. Lest there be any doubt concerning Engel's opinion as to the kind of Labour Party he would support at this stage in the history of the British working class, let Engels speak for himself. Writing in a letter to Sorge on November 29th, 1886, he said:

> 'The first great step in a country which enters the movement for the first time is to constitute the workers as an independent Labour Party, no matter in what way, so long as it is a distinct Labour Party . . . The masses need both time and opportunity to develop, and this opportunity they will obtain only on having a movement of their own – no matter in what form as long as it is their own movement – in which they will be driven forward by their own mistakes, and acquire wisdom by their failures.'[1]

But none of these attempts reached the masses. They had still to have this question forced upon them by experience.

Nevertheless this grouping of socialists had an important bearing upon the future of the coming Labour Party, whilst the sharp differences seen in the Social Democratic

[1] *From Chartism to Labourism*, by Th. Rothstein, p. 281.

Federation were the beginnings of a fateful policy which has repeatedly isolated the revolutionaries from the workers' movement. They antagonized the trade unions by the ferocity of their criticism. From a doctrinal point of view the S.D.F. was correct. Viewed historically it was wrong, and certainly contrary to the policy pursued by their teachers, Marx and Engels in the First International. Marx never made a frontal attack upon the trade unions such as the S.D.F. had made. To do so was fatal. Instead of the workers assimilating the message of the S.D.F., they resented it and isolated the revolutionaries who belonged to it. Had the S.D.F. regarded the class war as an historical process instead of idealizing it into a doctrinal yardstick with which to flog all those who did not agree with it; had it subordinated its criticism to the next practical steps to be taken in the preparation of the working class to become the ruling class it would have served the workers better. It would not have handed over the leadership to the reformists, the Liberals, Fabians, I.L.P. specialists and conservative trade union leaders. But the 'Marxism' of the S.D.F. was the 'Marxism' of Hyndman and not of Marx.

The disputes between the socialist groups did not help forward the cause of socialism. The S.D.F. at first regarded the I.L.P. as splitters and the relations between them were anything but friendly. It placed them both at a disadvantage in the struggle against the conservative and liberal politics of the trade union leaders, whilst the effect on the masses who had been divorced from political discussions for a long period was 'unfortunate' too. They regarded the disputes as quarrels between 'queer' people and socialism had to fight its way as a very unpopular cause.

CHAPTER IV

SELF-ISOLATION OF THE REVOLUTIONARIES

WHATEVER rejoicing there may have been in the ranks of the capitalists at the demise of the First International it must have been short-lived. Within a few years the working class of the European countries were busily engaged in re-constructing international organizations. In this movement the British workers were soon involved on a large scale, though the delay in forming a worker's political party in Britain marked the backwardness of British working-class politics.

In 1871 the Tobacco Workers' Union took the initiative in forming the Tobacco Workers' International Federation. In 1890 the British Miners' Federation took the initiative in establishing the International Miners' Federation, which has held an international Congress almost every year since that date. Between the years 1891 and 1897 the Woodworkers, Printers, Metal Workers, Textile Workers, Transport Workers, Potters and Furriers became part of their respective International Federation. In 1883 and 1886 the British Trades Union Congress sent delegates to International Congresses in opposition to the will of the Parliamentary Committee (the latter was the leading committee of the Congress) and forced it to be responsible for the convening of the International Congress of 1888. It was so opposed to the idea and so fearful of the presence of socialists that it imposed restrictions on representation. Despite this a majority of the delegates proved to be socialists including John Burns, Tom Mann, Keir Hardie and Mrs. Besant.

It was not until 1901 however that a General International of Trade Unions was established and became known as the Amsterdam International because its headquarters were in Amsterdam. These headquarters, as in the case of the sectional internationals, can hardly be described as anything more than the beginnings of centralization in international trades unionism. The duties of the International Secretariat were defined as being 'the maintenance of relations between the National Trade Union Federations and the compilation of a summary of the annual reports of the affiliated National Federations, and its publication in English, French and German.[1]

In 1889, the Socialist parties of Europe and Britain took a great step forward through the establishment of the Second International Working-men's Association. The most powerful party in the International was the German Social Democratic Party. This party, which claimed to be Marxist, held the leadership until the collapse of the Second International at the outbreak of war in 1914. The Second International was never a homogeneous organization. It was rather a collection of national parties representing conflicting currents of socialist opinion, all of which felt the common urge of the working class of Europe to get together. It was held together by an International Information or Corresponding Bureau.

The most important question at all its conferences was that of the coming war. From the first conference to the last before the outbreak of war, the socialists recognized

[1] *Labour Year Book*, 1924, p. 359.

that war was near. The conferences passed their resolutions but it cannot be said that there followed any realistic preparation to put the resolutions into life. There was propaganda in abundance, warnings galore, but no conclusive actions signifying preparedness. How could there be such preparation when the proletarian movement had not advanced so far towards international unity as to recognize the binding character of international resolutions, and while in some countries labour parties were in their infancy! The whole international movement was still saturated with liberalism, the first fruits of the epoch of capitalist expansion and imperialism. And none more so than the labour movement of Britain.

When, at the first Congress in 1889, it declared its intention of organizing international action for the eight-hour day, Engels hailed it joyfully and said how he wished that Marx could have lived to see the re-birth of the International. England was represented by the I.L.P., the Socialist League, the Social Democratic Federation and some trade union representatives. At this Conference the Anarchists were admitted, but at Zurich in 1893 they were excluded on the grounds that the Second International was a socialist international.

The principles of the International were formulated as follows:

1. The political and economic organization of the working class for the purpose of abolishing the capitalist form of society and achieving complete freedom for humanity through the conquest of political power and the socialization of the means of production and exchange, that is to say, by the transformation of capitalist society into a collectivist or communist society.

2. The international union and action of the workers in the struggle against jingoism and imperialism and for the simultaneous suppression of militarism and armaments, with the object of bringing about a real League of Nations, including all peoples master of their own destiny, and maintaining world peace.

3. The representation and defence of the interests of oppressed peoples and subject races. These principles find three forms of expression in the working class movement, each at different stages of development, but each necessary; the political, the industrial and co-operative. These must, as autonomous bodies, continue to strengthen their national influence, and their international unity. At the same time, as their ultimate aims are common, and as they are aspects of one great world movement they should take every opportunity for joint action in an internationalist and revolutionary spirit for the maintenance of world peace.

But there was no Labour Party of Britain to subscribe to these lofty principles. None of the parties from this country were yet more than small sects. The I.L.P. represented only a few thousand people. Composed largely of intellectuals and Christian Socialists, it had succeeded very little better than the S.D.F., which was also composed of intellectuals and a few workers, in attracting the masses into its ranks. It was not until 1908 that the young Labour Party made application for affiliation. It was then accepted with considerable doubts and fears. Bruce Glasier on behalf of the I.L.P. pleaded that though the Labour Party was not a socialist party it did carry on the class struggle. The S.D.F. with their characteristic sectarian outlook demanded the non-admission of the Labour Party until the latter recognized the class struggle and had a socialist aim.

Lenin favoured the admission of the Labour Party on the grounds:

> 'That the Labour Party in England is separated in Parliament (not at the elections! not in its whole policy! not in its agitation and propaganda!) from the bourgeois parties, is making the first step to socialism and a class policy, for the mass proletarian organization, is beyond dispute.'[1]

Before the British working-class movement reached this important stage big events had to take place in the experience of the working class. The trade unions had to be once again challenged by the ruling class before the mass break with Liberalism took place.

Following the great engineers' strike of 1897 and the strike of the Welsh miners in 1898 a number of law court decisions concerning picketing and collective responsibility shattered the Trade Union Acts of 1871 and 1876. What is known as the Taff Vale decision (1900–1) was a revelation of how far the rights of the trade unions had been taken away. This decision of the Law Courts ruled that a trade union could be made answerable in damages for all acts of its officials, central or local, as if it were a corporate body whilst still being denied the privileges of such a body. The Amalgamated Society of Railway Servants were sued for damages. They had to pay £23,000 and in a similar action the South Wales Miners had to pay £50,000.

[1] *Collected Works*, vol. xii, pp. 347–348.

It can hardly be a matter of surprise, therefore, that when James Holmes, organizer of the Taff Vale strike, moved the following resolution at the Trades Union Congress of 1899, it was passed by 546,000 votes to 434,000. The resolution reads:

> 'This Congress having regard to the decisions of former years, and with a view to securing better representation of the interests of Labour in the House of Commons, hereby instructs the Parliamentary Committee of the Trade Union Congress to invite the co-operation of all the Co-operative, Socialist, Trade Union, and other working-class organizations jointly to co-operate on lines mutually agreed upon in convening a special Congress of representatives from such of the above-mentioned organizations as may be willing to take part to devise ways and means for the securing of an increased number of Labour members to the next Parliament.'[1]

A special committee was appointed composed of representatives of the Parliamentary Committee of the T.U.C., the I.L.P., the S.D.F. and Fabian Society. This committee prepared a special congress of the organizations responding to the resolution of the T.U.C. On February 27th and 28th, 1900, one hundred and twenty delegates met in London to take the first steps in the formation of the Labour Party, 'the first step to socialism and a class policy for the proletarian organizations'.

These delegates represented half a million workers of the trade union and socialist organizations. They did not get further at this stage than the establishment of an

[1] Beer's *History of British Socialism*, p. 316.

organization known as the Labour Representation Committee. The decisive resolution says:

> 'That this Conference is in favour of establishing a distinct Labour group in Parliament, who shall have their own whips, and agree upon their policy, which must embrace a readiness to co-operate with any party which for the time being may be engaged in promoting legislation in the direct interest of labour, and be equally ready to associate themselves with any party in opposing measures having an opposite tendency.'[1]

The discussion on this resolution reveals once again the sectarianism of the revolutionary socialists. The S.D.F. put forward a resolution in which it demanded the 'recognition of the class war' and the ultimate object 'the socialization of the means of production, distribution and exchange'. At its next conference in 1901 the S.D.F. withdrew from the Labour Representation Committee and made way for Liberal-Labour trade union Leaders. They kept the doctrine pure for themselves but handed over the labour movement, at the very moment when there was a great influx of affiliations, to those who were opposed to class-war principles, in short to the Fabians, reformist socialists and liberals.

The influence of the S.D.F. thereby became more indirect. It had taken this organization sixteen years to recover from its violent denunciation of the trade unions only to isolate itself once more by this sectarian attitude to the Labour Representation Committee. Instead of bringing it nearer to the masses this latest development was but the prelude to new splits both on the question of trade unionism and of social reform. The

[1] Beer's *History of British Socialism*, p. 328.

split on the first question led to the formation of the Socialist Labour Party in 1903 and the split on the second issue led to the formation of the Socialist Party of Great Britain in 1905.

The forces of the S.L.P. were centred mainly in Scotland. This party was essentially a De Leon Party. De Leon was known as the most outstanding Marxist of America and was the leader of the Socialist Labour Party of America. The first prominent leader of the S.L.P. in Britain was James Connolly, the famous Irish Revolutionary Socialist.

The S.L.P. began a new current of thought in this country which has had a profound influence on all sections of the revolutionary movements and organizations which subsequently developed here. For the first time the theory of Industrial Unionism was expounded as the means to socialism. It had much in it of the ideas enunciated by James Morrison, the Chartist. Connolly expressed the theory and outlook of the S.L.P. most clearly in his pamphlet 'Socialism Made Easy'. He says, (p. 13).

> 'Industrial unity once established will create the political unity of the working class . . . It is an axiom enforced by all experiences of the ages that they who rule industrially will rule politically, and that, therefore, they who are divided industrially will remain impotent politically . . . natural law leads us as individuals to unite in our crafts, as crafts to unite in our industry, and as industries in our class; and this finished expression of that evolution is, we believe, the appearance of our class upon the political battle ground with all the economic power behind it to enforce its mandates.

'Until that day dawns *our political parties of the working class are propagandist agencies, John the Baptists of the New Redemption; but when that day dawns our political party will be armed with all the might of our class; will be revolutionary in fact as well as in thought.*'

'What the socialist does realize is that under a socialist form of society the administration of affairs will be in the hands of representatives of the various industries of the nation; that the workers in the shops and factories will organize themselves into unions, each union comprising all the workers of a given industry in subordination to the needs of its allied trades and to the department of industry to which it belongs. That representatives of the various departments of industry will meet and form the industrial administration or national government of the country.'

The S.L.P. had evidently learned something from the Paris Commune and recognized that the socialist order meant the 'administration of things' instead of class rule and class oppression. But its conception as to how this new state of society could be achieved constitutes an industrial form of 'gradualism' in striking contradiction to the teachings of Marx to which the S.L.P. was supposed to subscribe. Connolly explains the process, which was later called 'encroaching control', as a steady organization of each workshop and factory until all the factories are in the hands of the workers. He says,

'. . . In the light of this principle of Industrial Unionism every fresh shop or factory organized under its banner is a fort wrenched from the capitalist class and manned with the soldiers of the revolution to be held by them for the workers.

'On the day that the political and economic forces of labour finally break with capitalist society and proclaim the Workers' Republic these shops and factories so manned by Industrial Unionists will be taken charge of by the workers there employed and force and effectiveness given to that proclamation.'

It is as if all the revolutionary teaching of Marx and Engels concerning the nature and role of the capitalist state had been forgotten when strategical and tactical questions were being thought out; and this, despite the fact that the S.L.P. did more than any other party in this country to explain the 'Capitalist State as the Executive Committee of the Capitalist class'. It reduced the part played by a political party to that of a propaganda society instead of raising it to the forefront as the leader of the political struggle. The organization of the workers as industrial unionists became more important than the transformation of economic struggles into political struggles. The conquest of the state was reduced to the simple proposition of declaring a Workers' Republic by the working class organized one hundred per cent in industrial unions. Strange indeed that Connolly of all people, who later led the Irish insurrection of 1916, and met his death at the hands of the State, should be the pioneer and protagonist of this doctrine throughout his lifetime. Yet thus Connolly writes:

'This leads me to that last axiom of which I wish you to grasp the significance. It is this, *that the fight for the conquest of the political state is not the battle, it is only the echo of the battle.* The real battle is the battle being fought out every day for the power to control industry, and the gauge of the progress of the battle is not to be

> found in the number of voters making a cross beneath the symbol of a political party, but in the number of workers who enrol themselves in an industrial organization with the definite purpose of making themselves masters of the industrial equipment of society in general.'

What a contrast to the teachings of Marx in the name of Marx! Instead of the conquest of the political state being the 'echo of the battle', Marx sets this question before the proletariat as the first fundamental task of the revolution. 'Strictly speaking', he says in the 'Communist Manifesto', 'Political power is the organized use of force by one class in order to keep another in subjection . . . the first step in the workers' revolution is to make the proletariat the ruling class. . . .'

Nevertheless from this time forward the ideas expressed by Connolly are in the ascendancy in every revolutionary movement in Britain until after the Russian November Revolution of 1917. There is little difference in this outline of policy by Connolly to that of the Industrial Workers of the World, which also tried to secure a foothold in Britain in this period. The I.W.W. also stood for the industrial organization of the working class, but rejected the proposal for a workers' political party as unnecessary and reformist.

The I.W.W. met with no organizational success in this country. It was even more isolated from the British workers than the S.D.F. after its manifesto against trade unionism. The S.L.P. initiated an industrial unionist organization known as the Industrial Workers of Great Britain and tried to overcome its isolation by compromising on the question of leaving the trade unions. It permitted its members to retain their trade union membership until sufficient workers had been enrolled to enable the Industrial Union to supersede the trade unions. It demanded, however, that its recruits subscribe to the doctrine of the class war as a condition of membership. It never had more than 10,000 members.

The ideas they expressed were not limited to these organizations. There appeared in 1910 a further adaptation of the same theory to the realities of the trade union situation. The 'Syndicalist Education League' began the propagation of industrial unionism with a view to transforming the existing unions into industrial unions.

Under the chairmanship of A. A. Purcell, this organization called a conference of trade unionists in Manchester in the year 1910. There were one hundred and ninety-eight delegates present, representing seventy to eighty societies, groups and unions, and sixteen trades councils. Tom Mann, fresh from contact with the French syndicalists, dominated the conference. Supporting them were such well-known men as Ben Tillett, R. Coppock, now Secretary of the National Federation of Building Trades Operatives, Jim Larkin, J. Compton, Noah Ablett, and Peter Larkin.

A. A. Purcell, in his opening address said he

> 'looked upon industrial unionism as a movement which was more important than the political labour movement. The industrial workers themselves were the propelling force that would impel politics to what they desired them to be. This force was what was required to emancipate the workers if they were to be emancipated at all . . . The thing needed to emancipate the workers as a class, was not to federate but to amalgamate their movement to such an extent that whenever

> one worker was attacked, be he joiner, plasterer, labourer, shop assistant, etc., any attack upon any worker would be the signal for the resentment of the workers throughout the industrial world.'

The principal resolution of the conference endorsed this line, namely, the merging of all existing unions into one compact organization for each industry, including all labourers of every industry in the same organization as the skilled workers.

Their aversion to the question of the need for a workers' political party found expression in a special resolution in which the League decided to leave the question open to everyone to please himself as to his political alliance. Tom Mann said, 'It would be wise to go to America for guidance in this matter. When the Industrial Workers of the World was started in 1905 definite action – industrial and political – was decided on. But on the result of experience they revised their preamble at the Chicago Convention of 1908'. A resolution was then passed in the face of fierce opposition from De Leon in the following terms:

> 'That to the end of promoting unity and securing necessary discipline within the organization, the I.W.W. refuses all alliances, direct or indirect, with existing political parties or anti-political sects, and disclaims responsibility for any individual opinion or act which may be at variance with the purpose herein expressed.'

This meant that they were neither 'pro' nor 'anti-political' and that they took up an industrial position only.[1]

[1] *Industrial Syndicalist*, December, 1910.

The Industrial Syndicalist League existed for a few years and organized many such conferences in the most important industrial centres. Its programme added nothing to that outlined by Connolly in his statement for the Socialist Labour Party. Indeed, it was more limited, having nothing to say on politics whatever in this most important period when the working class was breaking from liberalism and forming its own political party.

The organization remained loose and entirely propagandist of this single idea of amalgamation of the unions into industrial unions on the basis of class-war doctrine. It achieved considerable influence and from it arose a number of efforts to apply its ideas in various industries. Amalgamation committees were formed in the metal, engineering and ship-building industries and the building industry. Miners' Reform Committees were formed in the miners' unions whilst a new movement, permeated through and through with De Leonist and syndicalist ideas, took shape in the form of the Plebs League and the Labour College Movement.

The origin and development of this latter movement have been fully described by J. F. and Winifred Horrabin in their book *Working-Class Education.* It arose as the result of a strike of students at Ruskin College in 1907, when the students protested against the exclusion of Marxist teachings from the curriculum. This movement represents both the deepening of revolutionary propaganda and the beginning of an organized effort to give class conscious form and content to the process of breaking the labour movement away from its class collaboration associations, by giving it a sounder theoretical grasp of its own class position in society.

The institutions engaged upon the task of giving the

new independent labour movement theoretical equipment were keen upon preserving and fostering the policy of class collaboration. Chief amongst these were the University Extension movement, the Workers' Educational Association and Ruskin College. The rise of the Plebs League and the students' strike broke this control over labour education and set the pace, through the agitation of the industrial unionists and the syndicalists, for *independent working-class education.*

Probably of more importance than the establishment of the Labour College itself has been the network of classes which spread widely throughout the country in the succeeding years, enrolling at one time not less than 20,000 students. At first only two unions came to their support. These were the South Wales Miners' Federation and the Railway Servants (later merged in the National Union of Railwaymen). Later, however, many more joined forces with them and established the National Council of Labour Colleges.

The programme of education and its publications give convincing evidence of the influence of the industrial unionists and the syndicalists. We read on p. 75 of *Working-Class Education* by the Horrabins, 'if then the primary aim of working-class education be to assist the workers in their class struggle against capitalism, the general methods by which this aim will be realized may be classified in four main groups:

1. Elementary education for the rank and file of the workers' movement, aiming at giving a sound grasp of broad essential facts and principles.
2. More advanced education for the minority who desire and are able, to carry their studies further.

3. The training of tutors.
4. The training in the technical details of their work, of trade union organizers and officials, labour propagandists, etc.

Elementary education is described as follows: 'The basis of this elementary education – as indeed of all workers' education – will be history; particularly the history of trade unionism and of the modern working-class movement, and the development of modern capitalism (imperialism, international problems, etc.). Such courses will be followed by the study of economics, economic geography, psychology, etc., the aim of the tutor being always to show clearly the inter-relation of all these subjects and above all else to the facts and problems of the everyday life of the workers. His chief task in short is to answer briefly but convincingly the three fundamental questions:

> 'What the present position of the workers as a class is. *How* and *why* it came to be so. *How* the workers can alter it.'

It will be observed that nothing is said here of class politics or of the role and history of political parties. To these questions the Labour College Movement adopted identically the same attitude as defined in the resolution quoted by Tom Mann at the Industrial Syndicalist Conference in 1910. But towards industrial unionism it has always been definite. Indeed, it has been one of the most potent weapons for the advancement of the theory of industrial unionism in the trade unions. This was done under the banner of Marxism but it was nearer to the Marxism of the syndicalists than to the Marxism of Marx.

Several of the students of the Labour College were

leaders of the miners' reform movement organized in South Wales and participated in the production of the 'Miners' Next Step'. This pamphlet, which contained a programme for the miners, created a great stir in the whole trade union movement.

Up to this time the industrialists and syndicalists had been content to rally their fellow workers behind any demands put forward by the respective unions and to concentrate their own proposals on questions of re-organization of the unions. The 'Miners' Next Step' gave a new turn to the campaigns of the revolutionaries. They now proceeded to work on the principle of uniting the workers by unifying the demands of the workers upon the employers, thus making the current issues of the struggle of vital importance to the question of union reorganization.

The programme outlined in the pamphlet consisted of a plan for 'One Union for the Mining industry, a demand for 8s. per day for all workers in and about the mines, and a seven hour day'. It also declared 'That the organization shall engage in political action, both local and national, on the basis of complete independence of and hostility to all capitalist parties, with an avowed policy of wresting whatever advantage it can for the working class . . . Alliances to be formed and trades union organization fostered with a view to steps being taken to amalgamate all workers' organizations into one national and international union, to work for the taking over of all industries by the workmen themselves'.

So far this is an application of the theory outlined by Connolly except that it dismisses the role of a political party altogether and leaps forward to the goal which he visualized, of the unions fulfilling all functions. Actually it was a step backward rather than forward.

But this is as nothing compared with the damage they wrought with the theory they advanced in relation to leadership. They proposed that 'all initiative for new proposals, policies and tactics remain with the lodge. Nothing becomes law in the organization unless it receives the sanction of the lodge or a ballot vote of the coal fields'. 'The Executive of the union,' they said, 'must be purely an administrative body deprived of all executive power.'

Of all theories that played straight into the hands of every reactionary executive, none has been more effective than this. It represents a complete abandonment of all responsibility for leaders to lead. Arising out of distrust of existing leaders, it fostered still further distrust, and at the same time gave them a first class excuse for not leading. This theory permeated all the 'left' sections of the movement, amalgamation committees, the shop stewards' movement of a later date, as well as the reform committees. It created an anti-official outlook of a character which stultified any real organized effort to replace reactionary leaders by revolutionary leaders. It diffused the energies of the revolutionaries and made their movement into a ferment rather than an organized force fighting for a new leadership.

Hence, right from the new beginnings of Revolutionary socialism in the 'eighties and 'nineties, Marxism was distorted. Decisive positions of influence were surrendered at the very moment that the masses advanced towards the formation of their own political party. Revolutionary influence was diffused and no means were created to translate this influence into the realities of leadership and organization. The working class had thus to advance to greater independence as a class, in spite of its revolutionary friends, under a leadership whose outlook was that of the capitalist class. Not one of the leaders responsible for the formation of the Labour Party regarded himself as a leader of a class destined to become the ruling class, but rather as the leader of a class finding a respectable place of dignified subordination to, and collaboration with other classes within capitalism, which the most advanced of them hoped to reform into socialism.

Each advance of the working class as a whole therefore has depended upon the growth of class contradictions at the foundations of capitalism which have forced masses and leaders into class actions despite their theories. The national concentration of unions had been rejected, but the concentration of industry and the struggles which ensued resulted in the formation of Trades Councils, the Trades Union Congress, and the General Federation of Trade Unions. The leaders of the Trades Union Congress rejected international organization. Pressure from below, following the rapid development of international capitalism, brought into being a network of international federations of the unions. Independent labour politics and parties were rejected by the great majority of the leaders and the masses for more than forty years. The intensification of the class struggle jeopardized the existence of the trade unions. From this arose the mass movement for the formation of the Labour Party. The lines of development indicated in the writings of Marx and Engels, crystallized in the 'Communist Manifesto' and the documents of the First International, were thus being fulfilled in spite of both their opponents and their friends.

The rise of the Labour Party corresponds with the beginning of a new period in the history of British capitalism. Real wages began to fall. The life of the working class became more harsh. New political attacks were made on the trade unions. Socialism received a great impetus. Having taken the first step in the organization of independent working-class politics, the Labour Representation Committee was quickly compelled to take the next step.

In the General Election of 1900 the L.R.C. had fifteen candidates. Two were successful – Richard Bell and Keir Hardie. In 1902 David Shackleton was returned unopposed at Clitheroe. In 1903 two by-elections resulted in the return of Will Crooks and Arthur Henderson.

The defection of Bell who returned to the Liberal Party, and the swamping of the Labour organizations with liberals who were still maintaining their old party loyalties, forced the National Conference of 1903 to make a change in the constitution completing the organizational break with the Liberal Party.

By 1906 the Labour Representation Committee was transformed into the Labour Party. Twenty-nine members were elected to Parliament the same year. The Taff Vale decision was reversed. At the 8th Annual Conference the following resolution, put forward only to test opinion, was passed by 514,000 votes to 469,000.

> 'That in the opinion of this Conference the time has arrived when the Labour Party should have as a definite object, the socialization of the means of production, distribution and exchange, to be controlled by a democratic State in the interest of the entire community; and the complete emancipation of labour from

the domination of capitalism and landlordism, with the establishment of social and economic equality of the sexes.'[1]

The acceptance of this resolution marks a decided advance from the politics of the old parties of capitalism.

Prior to this however, the Colne Valley by-election of 1907, demonstrated the growth of socialist opinion amongst the workers and gave one more example of the rank and file of the movement kicking the leaders forward. Colne Valley was a traditional Liberal seat. The Labour Representation Committee vetoed the proposal of the local workers' organizations to put an independent labour candidate in the field. The workers took matters into their own hands and not only nominated Victor Grayson as a socialist condidate, but secured his election.

This was followed in 1908 by the transformation of the Social Democratic Federation, with the addition of some dissident I.L.P. branches and the support of Blatchford and the *Clarion*, into the British Socialist Party.

The growth of the Labour Party on the basis of the trade unions, brought with it a new legal question – that of the use of trade union funds for political purposes. The Law Lords ruled that compulsory levies for this purpose were illegal and at one stroke the financial basis of the Labour Party was shattered. This was known as the Osborne judgment. It effectively slowed down the development of the Labour Party for some years. It was not until 1913 that a new Trade Union Act was passed permitting the payment of the political levy by the unions on the basis of a special ballot in the unions and the right of the individual to 'contract out'.

[1] Beer's *History of British Socialism*, p. 336.

But another important factor contributed to the slowing down of the growth of the Labour Party. It was at this time that Mr. Lloyd George conducted a great political manœuvre on behalf of the Liberal Party. Nobody recognized more clearly than he, that the rise of the Labour Party meant also the decline of the Liberal Party. It was this reading of history in the making, that led to the launching of his Limehouse campaign. He declared 'if a Liberal Government tackle the landlords, and the brewers, and the peers, as they have faced the parsons, and try to deliver the nation from the pernicious control of the confederacy of monopolists, then the independent Labour Party will call in vain upon the working men of Britain to desert Liberalism that is gallantly fighting to rid the land of the wrongs that have oppressed those who labour in it'.

This was the first but not the last manœuvre of Mr. Lloyd George to prevent the working class getting on to its own feet and developing its own political aims. Indeed, it is no exaggeration to say that it is the key to his whole political career. No man has been more conscious of the significance of the rise of the Labour Party. No man has more cleverly guided his class in its manœuvres to hold back the workers from socialism. At one moment he seeks to embrace the Labour Movement and bring it within the fold of the Liberal Party. At another he cries aloud for the unity of the Liberals and the Tories against the on-coming Bolshevik menace represented by the Labour Party. And then again he moves back to Limehouse.

This time the great manœuvre brought in its trail the Trades Dispute Act of 1906, the Workmen's Compen-

[1] Beer's *History of British Socialism*, p. 349.

sation Act of 1907, the Old Age Pensions Act of 1908, the Trade Boards Act of 1909, the Miners' Eight Hour Act 1908, the National Insurance Act of 1911, the Coal Mines Act of 1912 and the Trade Union Act of 1913. The two latter, however, were partly the result of the great strike wave which swept the working class forward during 1911 to 1913. Dockers and seamen, carmen, haulers, miners, railwaymen, were engaged in great conflicts. Many of the struggles started unofficially and drove the leaders into action.

The movement began amongst the transport workers who, under the inspiration of Tom Mann, Ben Tillet and others of the militant industrialists and syndicalists, had formed the Transport Workers' Federation. In 1911 they presented an ultimatum to the Employers' Association of the Port of London, with their demand for higher wages. Receiving no satisfaction, the transport workers, dockers and carters, tied up the Port of London with a strike far more complete than the strike of 1889 which had started the organization of the unskilled workers. The Government brought 25,000 soldiers into the port to act as strike breakers. Later the Government negotiated with the Federation and came to terms with the leaders. The workers rejected the terms and forced new ones.

Hardly had this storm subsided than a great railway strike began in Liverpool. Exasperated by the procrastination of the local railway company which delayed the calling together of the conciliation committee to examine their grievances, they downed tools. The strike spread rapidly to Manchester and other centres and a general clamour arose for the union executives to call a general strike on the railways. The four union executives involved joined it. This militant action succeeded. The unions multiplied in membership. It was this strike movement which led to the amalgamation of three of the four unions into the National Union of Railwaymen.

In 1912, a still greater shock was given to the capitalists by a general miners' strike lasting five weeks. Again it was preceded by fierce unofficial strikes. This time the storm centre was South Wales, where for twelve months 12,000 miners waged a fierce struggle in the teeth of the opposition of the union leaders and police protection for blacklegs. A number of these leaders who had opposed the extension of the strike, including Mr. Brace, Mr. Onions and Mr. Abrahams were defeated in the next elections to the South Wales Miners' Union Executive and replaced with revolutionary syndicalists.

Thus in the economic struggles as well as the political, the growing severity of class antagonisms was revolutionizing the masses and bringing them into conflict with their own leaders who were steeped in the politics of liberal prosperous capitalism.

But the greatest of all in its revolutionary significance, was the strike of the Dublin Transport Workers in 1913. This was led by James Larkin and James Connolly. It disclosed the terrible conditions of the Dublin proletariat and made such a terrific indictment of the Dublin employers, who, led by Mr. Martin Murphy, had determined to smash the Transport Union, that the whole working class of the British Isles were roused to a pitch of enthusiastic support of the strikers. The trade unions rallied to their support and for the first time on a big scale, the Co-operative Movement, now grown to a great trading concern, revealed its working-class content and sympathies, by sending ship loads of food from England to Dublin to feed the strikers and their dependents. Class solidarity stretched across the Irish Sea and blazed brightly through all the industrial centres of Britain. The masses of the British working class were finding the path of class independence and the voice of revolutionary socialism echoed throughout the country.

It was in this period that the *Daily Herald* was launched as the voice of militant socialism in the Labour Movement. Later the Labour Party officially launched the *Daily Citizen* but it was so tepid and uninspiring that it began to die immediately after it was born, although the lull in the development of the Labour Party had passed away and the trade unions were swept into its ranks.

A most notable product of these struggles was the formation of the Triple Alliance of Miners, Railwaymen and Transport Workers, embracing 1,500,000 workers. It was the biggest thing yet seen in the history of working-class combination.

It may be thought that the Trades Union Congress made such an organization unnecessary. But the T.U.C. was not yet a powerful combination. It was more of a parliament of the unions for mutual discussion than a combination for mass action.

It was controlled by a Parliamentary Committee of liberal trade unionists who did their best to prevent the T.U.C. from becoming an effective instrument of struggle. Had it been such an instrument the Triple Alliance would not have been formed. This alliance was a transitory phenomenon which was superseded after its collapse on Black Friday, 1921, by the formation of the General Council of the Trades Union Congress. But at the time of its appearance it certainly alarmed the capitalist class and was regarded by them as a portent of coming revolutionary struggles.

The fear was not unwarranted. By this time working-class organization was a factor to be reckoned with. Revolutionary socialism was spreading amongst the workers. The working class generally was more class conscious than at any time since the collapse of the Chartist Movement. Its organized power was greater than at any time in its history. And yet the leadership was liberal-labour, the revolutionary socialist parties were little sects, and the industrial unionists and syndicalists were lost amongst the mass of working-class organizations.

CHAPTER V

RISE OF THE SHOP STEWARDS

PROBABLY nothing reveals the political infancy of the revolutionary socialists and syndicalists at this time more than their utter helplessness at the outbreak of war. Amalgamation Committees, Reform Committees, Labour Colleges, and Plebs League muttered that it was 'outside their province' and 'the membership of each organization would have 'to take individual responsibility for their actions'. Those who were members of political parties such as the Socialist Labour Party, the British Socialist Party and the Independent Labour Party followed the lead of their respective parties.

The Socialist Labour Party denounced the war as an imperialist war and advised its members to refuse to serve in the army, and to declare that the only war for which they would enlist was the class war. In practice it meant that the members of the S.L.P. became conscientious objectors on the basis of the class war theory while a considerable section of the B.S.P. and the I.L.P. were conscientious objectors on pacifist grounds.

It is certainly true that the conscientious objectors' movement succeeded in focusing a considerable body of opinion against the war. But it is also true that it kept the army and navy free from the anti-war elements, free from the propagandists of the class war, in a more effective way than if the Government had designed a plan for the purpose. It left the armed forces totally dependent upon their own reactions to the war and without the guidance of any revolutionary leadership. There is no evidence of the existence at that time of any attempt to permeate the armed forces with revolutionary ideas.

Those who were not involved in the conscientious objectors' campaign, carried on a great deal of anti-war agitation in the factories. None were more active in this direction than the Socialist Labour Party and the British Socialist Party. The latter had survived a split on the question of supporting the war. Hyndman its former leader and a few others who were expelled, formed the Nationalist Socialist Party, which later re-named itself the Social Democratic Federation. The I.L.P. was divided. A good proportion of its members were conscientious objectors. Others carried their pacifist propaganda into the workshops. Officially, it conducted a campaign for peace by negotiation. Many of its members served on the social committees set up by the Government.

There was little if any organized opposition to the war. A great deal had been said about the coming war by the various parties. Many were looking for the trade unions to call for strike action. There was undoubtedly a strong feeling in the ranks of the workers against any war. All of the parties and the trade unions, as part of the Second International, were pledged to the Basle Resolution of 1910. This resolution said

> 'If war threatens to break out, it is the duty of the working classes and their parliamentary representatives in the countries involved, supported by the co-ordinating activity of the International Socialist Bureau, to exert every effort in order to prevent the outbreak of war by the means they consider most effective which naturally vary according to the sharpening of the class

struggle and the sharpening of the general political situation.

'In case war should break out anyway, it is their duty to intervene in favour of its speedy termination and with all their powers to utilize the economic and political crisis created by the war to arouse the people and thereby to hasten the downfall of capitalist class rule. . . .'

But very little happened. A manifesto was issued over the signatures of Henderson and Hardie which was an anti-war manifesto. There were big demonstrations in Trafalgar Square and some of the large cities. The Labour Party Executive renounced responsibility for the war and promptly proceeded to do its utmost to assist in its prosecution. The working class had once more to pay the penalty for having a leadership which actually functioned as the 'left-wing' of the capitalist class.

The General Federation of Trade Unions heartily supported the war. The Trades Union Congress, through its Parliamentary Committee, pledged the trade unions to see the war through. The I.L.P., whose leaders were also the leaders of the Labour Party, issued a manifesto in which it said, 'up to the last moment we laboured to prevent the blaze. The nation must now watch for the first opportunity for effective intervention. As for the future we must begin to prepare our minds for the difficult and dangerous complication that will arise at the conclusion of the war. . . .'

By the end of August, 1914, the National Labour Party Executive agreed to support the Government's recruiting campaign. Mr. MacDonald, who resigned from the leadership of the Labour Party as a gesture, wrote to his constituency advising the young men to join up. In a short time the Labour Party trade union leaders were fully supporting the Government. All their pledges to international socialism proved to be worthless. They made not the slightest effort to mobilize the workers against the war.

By August 24th, 1914, the Joint Board of the Trades Union Congress, the General Federation of Trade Unions and the Labour Party passed the following resolution:–

> 'That an immediate effort be made to terminate all existing disputes, whether strikes or lock-outs, and wherever new points of difficulty arise during the war a serious attempt should be made by all concerned to reach an amicable settlement before resorting to strikes or lock-outs.'

A sudden hush came over the whole movement after the universal capitulation. From January to July, 1914, the aggregate duration of all disputes totalled 9,105,800 working days. From August to December of the same year the total amounts to only 1,039,000 days.

The immediate effect of the war was to put a damper on industry. Unemployment grew by leaps and bounds. The cost of living increased. The unions, which had been striving to increase wages because of this tendency developing before the outbreak of war, found themselves in an increasingly difficult situation in view of their agreement to maintain 'industrial peace'. It soon became evident too, that the employers welcomed the new patriotism and used it as a means to resist wage advances which they would otherwise have approached more tolerantly. The slogan of the new patriotism was 'work for low wages and higher profits'.

The effect on the workers was seen in the increase of strikes. From January to July, 1915, they mounted up again to 2,333,700 days. None of these disputes were political disputes directed against the war but economic disputes. Nevertheless they show that the capitalist class was greatly indebted to the leaders of the British Labour Movement. Had the latter carried out the spirit of their own pledges to organize opposition to the war they could have found much material in the conditions and outlook of the workers to make such opposition. It was obvious however that they had become part of the war machine.

The engineering workers in particular were in a difficult position owing to the absurd practice of making local agreements on wages terminate at different dates. The Glasgow engineers for example were working on an agreement due to terminate at the beginning of 1915. This agreement accorded to the skilled engineers 8½d. per hour. On December 7th, 1914, a month's notice was served on the employers by the district committee of the Amalgamated Society of Engineers demanding 2d. per hour increase to bring their rate up to the level of other districts by the week ending January 13th, 1915.

The employers were ready and began manœuvring with negotiation machinery to delay matters. The district committee of the A.S.E. resented the tricks of the employers and issued instructions to their members to down tools on January 20th failing an adequate offer from the employers. The latter finally agreed to a conference on the 19th. After five hours' discussion the workers were offered ½d. per hour increase immediately, and another ½d. per hour in three months' time. This was rejected. On the 22nd the employers proposed ¾d.

per hour immediately. The conference lasted fifteen minutes.

The degree of restraint on the part of the workers was really remarkable. They permitted the question to be referred to a national conference to be held on February 12th, although their original application was made early enough to have been considered on January 15th. But they took action on the question of overtime and refused to work overtime on war contracts. An unofficial mass meeting demanded an immediate stoppage.

Here it is necessary to call a halt, for we are on the threshold of a new development. For the first time we witness a new movement taking the responsibility for independently leading the workers against the will of the established executives of the unions. The 'unofficial' mass meeting of Clyde engineers marked the progress from 'pressure upon the executives' to 'action in spite of the executives'. This is the moment when a new leadership arises from the struggle elected on the basis of a new franchise. The 'Shop Steward' stepped forward from his subordinate role to the actual leadership of the fight.

Of course, the principle of electing shop stewards was not new. The printers for example had elected the 'father of the chapel' through many generations. The Amalgamated Society of Engineers had recognized shop stewards for many years. But for the leadership of a district to pass into their hands was new indeed. Up to this date they had been subordinate to the district committee of the union. This committee was elected by ballot vote of the union branches. The branches of the unions are composed of trade unionists organized according to residential convenience. The shop stewards were elected by *vote of the workers inside the workshop*. The 'unofficial' mass meeting here referred to was organized by shop stewards of various workshops coming together and forming a representative committee for the purpose.

This new manifestation in the forms of struggle is important from another point of view. With it came the re-emergence of the revolutionary industrialists, amalgamationists, the socialists of the S.L.P., the B.S.P. and I.L.P. who were opposed to the war. John MacLean of the B.S.P. was the most prominent figure in the anti-war agitation on the Clyde and associated himself with the shop stewards in their struggles. These revolutionary elements now began to dominate the disputes throughout the war period.

The mass meeting on this occasion was only the first step towards independent action. It did not immediately declare the strike but demanded that the District Committee should do so. The latter, however, reinforced by the executive of the union, convened an 'official' mass meeting at which two executive members appealed for the resumption of overtime work on the ground that the stoppage would 'prejudice their demand'. The men re-affirmed their demand for the full 2d. per hour increase and refused to be intimidated.

The executive of the union still opposed the men. They agreed to the employers' offer of $\frac{3}{4}$d. per hour and decided to submit the terms to ballot, the papers to be returned a month later, i.e., March 9th.

The men felt insulted and on February 6th, led by the shop stewards, began to walk out of the workshops. By the end of the month more than half of the Clyde engineers were on the streets. A committee was set up by the shop stewards called 'The Labour Withholding Committee'. It insisted upon the full demands of the men and that the dispute 'shall be settled through this committee and not the union officials'.

But the shop stewards and the men continued to use the union machinery. All regarded themselves as loyal members of the union and justified their action on the ground that the union officials were no longer free agents. The ballot of the A.S.E. proceeded and turned down the proposals of the employers by 8,927 votes to 829.

Then came government intervention, which was regarded by the executive of the union as a command to resume work, and it urged the men to obey. The Labour Withholding Committee held the reins in their hands and insisted on terms. It was not until eight days later that they agreed to return to work after the Government had conceded 1d. per hour increase and made the payment retrospective as from February 15th. This advance was defined as a 'war bonus', depending on the operation of war conditions.

Behind this decision lay the precedent established by the National Union of Railwaymen and the Associated Society of Locomotive Engineers and Firemen, who had both accepted a 'war bonus'. This meant that from this time forward all changes in wage rates and conditions were to be regarded as temporary. The concession to the Clyde engineers was therefore put in a precarious condition. Their demand had nothing to do with war time conditions. Had the 2d. per hour been conceded they would have then only been brought up to the level of other districts. But they received only half of this and the employers could demand that it be revised again at the termination of the war.

The immediate effect, however, was to enhance the position of the shop stewards who had proved their ability to lead the struggle whilst the officials had proved their willingness to act as tools of the Government. Thus the workshop became the storm centre of militant activity. New leaders came to the front in Glasgow, MacManus, Gallacher, Kirkwood, Muir and Messer were the most prominent amongst them.

Immediately after this stormy introduction the Labour Withholding Committee turned its attention to the widening of the basis of the organization. It sought to increase the number of shop stewards and to unite the workers in the workshop on a class basis instead of on a craft basis. It proceeded to form workshop committees representative of all the workers and elected by them. Each shop had its convener of stewards, or leading steward, who had the right to pass from department to department according to the requirements of the shop stewards, to lead deputations to the management, etc. It changed its name to the Clyde Workers' Committee.

It must not be thought that these activities were directed against the trade unions. As a matter of fact they became the greatest recruiting agents for the unions. The shop stewards elected in the workshop received the endorsement of the union branches and committees.

The moment of the February dispute was not only the moment when the workers awoke to a new form of activity. It was also the moment of the great awakening of the ruling class of this country to the magnitude of the task upon which they had embarked. Now began three lines of policy in relation to industry. First, the transfer of labour into the engineering industry and its re-equipment for war purposes. Second, the centralization of everything into the hands of the State, the speed up of industry and its adaptation to military requirements.

Third, the binding of the unions to the government machine as the means of effectively repressing the workers.

After the stagnation of industry at the outbreak of war and the indiscriminate recruiting came the alarm which swept a mighty army into the engineering industry. Workers who had hitherto been accustomed to the textile industries found themselves taking railway tickets for the armament centres. Jewellery workers of Birmingham, publicans and friends of publicans were suddenly turned into munition workers. Women by the thousands and tens of thousands, left their homes and domestic service, donned the overalls of mechanics and responded to the call for munitions. Short time gave place to overtime and all kinds of schemes to keep the machinery going twenty-four hours per day and seven days per week.

On February 4th, 1915, the Government appointed a committee on Production in Engineering and Shipbuilding establishments 'to inquire and report forthwith, after consultation with representatives of employers and workmen, as to the best steps to be taken to ensure' increased production.

By March 5th the reports were available. On March 17th, 1915, the famous Treasury conference was held at which Mr. Lloyd George met the trade union leaders in conference. He got them to agree, apart from the Miners' Federation of Great Britain, that 'there shall in no case be a stoppage of work upon munitions and equipment of war or other work required for a satisfactory completion of the war'.

The Miners' Federation led by Robert Smillie were unwilling to accept compulsory arbitration and refused to have anything to do with the agreement after the first day's proceedings.

Then came a further step towards the consolidation of the Government and the Labour forces for the prosecution of the war. The Liberal Government resigned. A Coalition Government was established with three Labour men in the Government, namely, Mr. Henderson, Mr. Brace of the Miners' Federation, and Mr. Roberts. The International resolutions against war were now entirely forgotten. Instead of doing their utmost to end the war the Labour leaders did their utmost for the prosecution of a flagrantly imperialist war.

Within three months the Treasury Agreement was elaborated and compulsory powers increased by the passing of the Munitions Act of June, 1915. This provided, in addition to the terms already embodied in the Treasury Agreement, for Munition Tribunals, before which workers could be prosecuted for losing time or other misdemeanours. By August the system of 'leaving certificates' was established and no worker employed on war work could leave his employment without a certificate of permission from his employer.

In September, a Joint Committee, representing the National Labour Advisory Committee and the Ministry of Munitions, with additional members, was appointed to advise and assist the Ministry in regard to the transfer of skilled labour and the introduction of semi-skilled and unskilled labour for munition work.

Before these measures were put fully into operation a crisis arose in the mining industry. Nearly twenty thousand miners had been drained into the army since the beginning of hostilities. Suddenly the Government woke up to the importance of coal. It sent up a cry for greater production. The mine owners demanded the reduction of 'avoidable absenteeism', the curtailment of holidays, the suspension of the Eight Hours Act, the introduction of 'diluted labour', the employment of women on pit head work, the reduction of the age limit at which boys were permitted to work in the mines, in short the abrogation of everything which the trade unions had fought for. And the cost of living was rising.

The miners opposed the demands of the mine owners, retaliated with the demand for a 20 per cent increase of wages and refused to have anything to do with arbitration. An awkward situation for the Government was avoided by the granting of concessions on wages. But an acute situation remained in South Wales where a district conciliation agreement terminated on April 1st. The South Wales Miners' Federation had given the necessary three months' notice for a new agreement. The owners refused to negotiate. A deadlock ensued. The men decided to strike. The strike was 'proclaimed' under the Munitions Act. The strikers returned the compliment and 'proclaimed' the Act. There were two hundred thousand strikers. In a week the strikers won. There was a new agreement and the Munitions Act remained a dead letter so far as the miners were concerned.

In this fight the Miners' Reform Committees played a prominent part by organizing great pressure within the union. The leaders of this movement were almost in control of the South Wales Miners' Federation. This was clearly shown when the Executive of the Federation on July 12th tried to prevent the strike occurring and pleaded for a continuation of work. It was A. J. Cook, Noah Abblett, W. Mainwaring and those associated with the Reform Committees and the Labour College Movement who led the attack against this policy and succeeded in driving the Executive into action. But these revolutionaries had no contact with the Clyde group.

Meanwhile dilution of Labour was proceeding apace in the engineering industry. The Munitions Act began to be operated. The War Office forced the pace with its recruiting schemes of 'single men first', married men to follow, according to age. The joint activity of the War Office and the Ministry of Munitions established industrial conscription as a fact. A worker could not leave one job for another without the permission of the employer. In the event of him having no job he was automatically eligible for the army.

The Clyde Workers' Committee countered the measures of the Government with a big agitation for the control of dilution. The shop stewards told their fellow workers plainly that they would be in a hopeless position if they entertained the delusion that there was any possibility of a return to pre-war conditions. Assisted by the revolutionary socialists such as John MacLean, MacDougal and Maxton the Clyde Workers' Committee took up a variety of issues such as the rent question as well as their factory campaign concerning the dilution of labour, as part of a big anti-war campaign. On the question of the fight against the increase of rents by the landlords the Clyde workers scored their greatest victory of the war period. A great rent strike was organized in which the women proved themselves to be great organizers of street pickets. The landlords tried to overcome the resistance of the workers to the payment of increased rents by bringing them into the debt court. Immediately the first workers appeared before the magistrate it was the signal for thousands of workers to leave the factories to attend the court. Tremendous demonstrations took place. The Ministry of Munitions intervened. The workers under arrest were released and the Government hurried through the Rent Restriction Act which to a large extent is still in force.

The Government saw that they would have to come to grips with the Clyde Movement which was becoming increasingly revolutionary. Mr. Lloyd George decided to tackle the job himself with a view to pushing through the policy of dilution. In December, 1915, he appeared in Glasgow accompanied by Lord Murray and Mr. Henderson. They determined to operate through the trade union officials.

As soon as the Clyde Workers' Committee heard of this visitation they determined that the war 'trinity' should receive a deputation from the committee and only be permitted to hold meetings with the workers under the control of the shop stewards. Hence immediately Mr. Lloyd George began a tour through the factories he found that shop stewards were preceding him and when he arrived at the factories the shop stewards there would not meet him. They were determined to force him to meet the Clyde Workers' Committee. In this they succeeded.

The delegation of twenty-six workers appointed J. W. Muir as their spokesman. Addressing Mr. Lloyd George and his colleagues he said,

> '. . . . . . we have sufficient intelligence not to need any lecturing on the question of the urgency of supplies for military and domestic purposes, and, what is more, we have very strong views on how they can best be obtained. There is no need either to take up any time

explaining to us the principles of the dilution of labour. . . . In short it is a step in the direct line of industrial evolution. But – and this is where the present difficulties arise – its progressive character is lost to the community unless it is accompanied by a corresponding step in social evolution. . . .

'. . . trouble can be averted by making the scheme conform *now* to certain conditions which I will specify. These are, that the benefits shall not acrue to one class in the community; that it shall not react detrimentally on any grade of labour; that organized labour must have a share in controlling it.

'These conditions can be fulfilled by the Government's compliance with the demands of the Clyde Workers' Committee that all industries and national resources must be taken over by the Government – not merely controlled – but taken over completely and that organized labour should be vested with the right to take part directly and equally with the present managers in the management and administration in every department of industry. I have used the term 'demand' advisedly as this is no propagandist statement. It is a fixed determination to force the matter to an issue . . . By its adoption the coming fight on conscription would be avoided – because conscription would be absolutely unnecessary. Whatever the Government do the Clyde Workers' Committee are going to devote themselves to fighting for the policy outlined.'[1]

This speech did not challenge the war. It demanded a price for carrying on the war, namely – 'the control of dilution by the workers engaged in industry on terms

[1] *The Worker*, No. ii.

which would not be detrimental to the workers in general and especially the skilled workers, whose position was being shattered by dilution'. The bold challenge to the Government to socialize industry and the 'fixed determination of the Committee to force the matter to an issue' was either window dressing propaganda or a complete over-estimation of the power and extent of the influence of the Clyde Workers' Committee.

But the terms of the speech were not so important as the actions of the movement at this juncture. The meeting of Mr. Lloyd George and his colleagues with six thousand workers in St. Andrew's Hall following the meeting with the delegation, ended in uproar. In fact the Government's delegation could hardly be described as a success.

The Government now decided to take repressive measures. A series of incidents took place without the Clyde Workers' Committee acting promptly and decisively.

In January of 1916 only a week or so after Mr. Lloyd George's stormy visit, the convener of shop stewards at Dalmuirs was discharged. A 'stay in' strike was started by his mates in the shop. The Munitions Act was brought into operation. Forty men were fined but nothing happened as a consequence. The C.W.C. gave no lead. The first prosecution under the Act was thus allowed to pass unchallenged.

The C.W.C. issued a weekly paper called *The Worker*. The military authorities came down on it with a rush. It was suppressed after four issues. J. W. Muir, the editor, W. Gallacher, the chairman of the C.W.C. and J. Bell, the business manager of the Socialist Labour Press which printed the paper, were arrested. Bail was not allowed at first but an immediate spontaneous strike made the authorities change their minds and bail was allowed. Some of the shops were in favour of continuing the strike until they had secured unconditional release of the arrested men. The C.W.C. recommended, however, that work be resumed.

The trial was fixed for April 14th. A further measure was then taken by the employers. Beardmores (Parkhead Forge) introduced a new rule prohibiting the leading shop stewards the right of visiting other departments than that in which they were employed. On March 17th, the workers of Beardmores walked out.

The Parkhead engineers issued a manifesto calling for the support of other workers. The Clyde Workers' Committee was silent and the strike did not extend to more than 10,000 men. The Government acted promptly and one night during the following week MacManus, Kirkwood, Messer, Wainwright, Haggerty and Shields, six of the leading shop stewards, were arrested and deported from the district.

But the Clyde Workers' Committee did nothing. The Parkhead men were left to extend the strike as best they could. With divided councils prevailing, and the trade union officials appealing to them to return to work on the plea that if the strike was called off their committee would be brought back, the strike collapsed. The deportees did not come back. They were taken to Edinburgh and later permitted to choose some place other than Glasgow in which to live and work.

In a statement made by representatives of the Clyde Workers' Committee presented to the Labour Party Court of Enquiry, set up to investigate the circumstances of the deportation, there is a remarkable light shed on the state of mind prevailing in the Clyde Workers' Committee at the time. It contrasts strongly with the bold speech of Muir before Lloyd George. The report says:

> 'At the C.W.C. meeting held in the Scottish Tinplate Workers' Hall, Watson Street, on March 25th, 1916, it was reported that the engineering workers of Parkhead Forge had been on strike since March 17th. It was also reported at this meeting that certain men employed at the Forge and at Messrs. G. and J. Weirs', Cathcart, had been arrested. The men were Kirkwood, Shields, and Haggerty of the Forge, and MacManus and Messer of Weirs. Later in the proceedings, it was reported that these men were to be deported from the Clyde area and some members of the C.W.C. left the meeting to see them off at the station.
>
> 'At this meeting, it was quite evident that the members were very indignant against the action of the Government. So keen was the indignation that a motion was submitted that the C.W.C. should declare a strike in the Clyde District. The chairman, William Gallacher, ruled this motion out of order as it was against the accepted aims of the C.W.C. This aim was the building of one industrial organization in the engineering industry. The members of the committee could inform their fellow workers in the shop where they worked as to what happened at the Forge, but beyond this the C.W.C. had no jurisdiction. No further discussion about the possibility of a strike took place at this meeting. . . .'

A strange document from a committee that was born in strike action and only a few weeks before were threatening the Government with social revolution!

The deportees were not alone in having to pay the

price for this policy of dependence upon spontaneous action and abandonment of leadership indicated in the ruling of Gallacher and accepted by the Committee. Work had only just been resumed when Gallacher, Muir and Bell came up for trial. The charge against them was 'that they printed or caused to be printed, an article entitled "Should the Workers Arm?" '

The most striking feature about this article, is the fact that it is directed against the arming of the proletariat and puts the industrialist position as the alternative. Its most 'violent' passage reads:

> 'The attack of the masters must be resisted. The workers must fight. What shall the weapon be? . . . There is a fascinating attraction in the idea of meeting force with force, violence with violence . . . If the internal clash of armed forces can be avoided in this country it should be avoided. There is another method, which if conducted on a thorough scale, should prove completely successful . . . To be effective the workers must organize as workers. An organization that would include all the workers, skilled and unskilled throughout the entire Clyde area would prove irresistible.'

If this is not a repudiation of military arms and an affirmation of the peaceful industrialist acquisition of power through one hundred per cent organization of the workers in industry, it would be interesting to know what is. There is not a paragraph in the whole four issues of the *Worker* more 'insurrectionary' than these. Nevertheless, Gallacher and Muir were sentenced to twelve months' imprisonment and Bell to three months. It is impossible to avoid the conclusion that these men were put away for their activities as leaders and not for the article. For advocating a strike at a neighbouring workshop gate to secure the release of the three, another worker named Jack Smith received eighteen months' imprisonment.

And nothing happened. The workers were leaderless. The Clyde Workers' Committee got out a petition drafted by the defending solicitor, Mr. Rosslyn Mitchell, which received 70,000 signatures, but without effect.

During the early months of 1916, John MacLean had been sentenced to three years imprisonment for seditious speeches. Maxton and MacDougal were each sentenced to one year in prison for similar offences. The back of the Clyde Movement was thus effectively broken for months to come. It had been essentially a local movement. But similar conditions in industry gave rise to a similar movement in the industrial centres of England.

CHAPTER VI

SHOP STEWARDS' MOVEMENT EXTENDS

THE centre of the struggle was now moved to Sheffield. Here, as in other engineering towns, there were shop stewards, but few in number. The great influx of unskilled and semi-skilled workers under the dilution schemes roused the skilled workers to great activity. Every trade union branch meeting saw scores of complaints brought forward, all of which were forwarded to the district committee of the unions. These were literally overwhelmed with complaints.

It was the study of these experiences which led the writer to bring forward proposals for workshop organization. These proposals were first discussed in the amalgamation committee. They were then brought forward in the Sheffield No. 8 Branch of the A.S.E. This was necessary in order to get the matter raised before the district committee of the union.

It was proposed that every branch of the union should make a registration of its members under the auspices of the district committee. This registration secured the information concerning the place of employment of every member of the union in the district and the number of shop stewards in every workshop. The district committee, on the basis of this registration had to undertake a systematic attack on each factory, until every factory wherein there were members of the A.S.E., had its quota of shop stewards. The other skilled workers' unions, such as the

Steam Engine Makers' Society, the Toolmakers, the Machine Workers' Union and the Pattern Makers' Society began to do likewise. This paved the way for the election of workshop committees representing all the shop stewards in each workshop.

The district committee of the A.S.E. was the first to adopt the plan. The executive of the union endorsed it. The campaign was soon in full swing. The drive of the members of the amalgamation committee in the other unions helped considerably to get these unions on the move too.

In a few months the factories of Sheffield were covered with a network of workshop committees. Towards the end of the year 1916 a new local crisis was created by the action of the local military authorities. Each of the government departments was working at top pressure. The military authorities were wanting men. The Munitions Department were wanting munitions. The latter, along with the unions, had arranged a system whereby those who were required for munition work were given a certificate and a badge, the possession of which was supposed to exempt them from military service.

But the military authorities were keen on sorting out the men and continually testing and re-testing their claims to exemption from military service. It was the enthusiasm on the part of the military officer in the Sheffield area that created a situation which stimulated all the union activities within the factories. A young skilled worker was taken into the army in flat contradiction to the regulations and agreements entered into with the trade unions. His claims had been ignored. He had been employed at Vickers, Ltd., and the case was reported to the shop stewards' committee who promptly gave great publicity to it throughout the workshops of the district.

The ordinary means of trade union negotiation were used without result. Communications received simply formal acknowledgement. It was obvious that the case would be lost unless something drastic was done immediately. The feeling on the question was acute. The men felt that if the military authorities were allowed to triumph at this stage they would be beaten all along the line. The unskilled workers also were not unsympathetic to the claims of the skilled workers because of their powerful propaganda and activity in defence of the unskilled workers' conditions.

Hence, on November 8th, 1916, the district committee of the A.S.E. and the shop stewards called a mass meeting of engineers and invited the skilled workers of other unions to attend. Here came the next step in the development of the independent leadership of the shop stewards. Whilst the district committee of the A.S.E. was present in full force, it retired from the leadership on the grounds that the district committee as part of the union machine was bound by the agreements as to strikes, etc. They passed the control into the hands of the shop stewards committee. This was possible because the majority of the members of the district committee were also shop stewards.

The response of the men was unanimous and determined. After a report on the details of what had been done and considerable discussion, a resolution was put to the effect that the Government be given one week in which to return the worker named Hargreaves, to his job as a civilian engineering worker on the same terms as the rest of his fellow engineers. Failing the return of the man within the specified time work would cease in the engineering factories of Sheffield until he did return.

The Prime Minister, the Ministry of Munitions, the War Office, the Trade Union Executives – all were notified the following day. The union executives with the exception of the Patternmakers' Association[1] simply gave formal acknowledgement to the communications. The Government answered not a word.

The day after the mass meeting the shop stewards' committee sent delegates to the principal engineering centres to inform the engineers throughout the country and urge them to be ready for action too.

On November 15th, the day when the ultimatum expired the whole organization was keyed up for action. It had been agreed that all the shop stewards on the night shift should meet during the afternoon in the Engineers' Institute and if no satisfactory reply from the Government arrived by 4 p.m. the strike would be promptly called and they would immediately proceed to the factories, inform the stewards on the day shift and prevent the night shift from starting work.

There were not less than two hundred shop stewards waiting for the stroke of four on this eventful day. Stand-

[1] Letter from Patternmakers' Association.

November 10*th*, 1916.

To Mr. J. T. Murphy.

Sheffield Engineers and Shop Stewards Committee.

Dear Sir, – In reply to yours of yesterday, I have no communication from any of our branches with regard to the position taken on the 'debadging' question and certainly no application has been received for permission to 'down tools' if a member of the A.S.E. is not immediately released from the army. Our position with regard to both the general and particular question is that we have accepted the Treasury Agreement which means that no strike must take place during the war, but that all disputes must be submitted to arbitration, so if our members come out on strike they will do so on their own responsibility and at their own cost. Your six days ultimatum to the Government is the most foolish and short-sighted action I have ever heard of.

Yours faithfully,

W. Mosses.

ing outside the Institute was a fleet of motor cycles with their cyclist shop stewards ready to be dispatched to the engineering centres, visited the previous week-end.

It was arranged that several should go southwards by different routes to cover Lincoln, Gainsborough, Nottingham, Leicester, Rugby, Bedford, London. Others were to go by Derby, Coventry, Birmingham, Rugby, London. Whilst these were to go southwards, others were to go to Manchester, Liverpool, Bolton, St. Helens, Barrow. Another group were to go to Leeds, Huddersfield, Halifax, Bradford, Keighley. And yet others were to go straight to Newcastle and the East Coast towns, northward to Edinburgh and Glasgow.

In all cases arrangements were made to reinforce them by delegates going by train who were to stay in the big centres under instructions not to return until directly instructed by the shop stewards' committee. This step was taken as a precaution against the press, in anticipation of the contradictory reports which they would undoubtedly issue concerning the strike.

Four o'clock came. The Government had not replied. The strike was called. The shop stewards rushed to the factories. The cyclists went off at once. At five o'clock the strike was complete. Ten thousand skilled workers walked out of the factories. Then the Government got busy with the telegraph wires.

The following day after great enthusiastic mass meetings of the strikers the following telegram was received by the writer :

'Reference to your letter to Prime Minister of November 9th, Minister Munitions is informed by the Executive Council Amalgamated Society of Engineers that they have telegraphed branch secretary as follows: On representation of Executive and in view of proposals submitted by Ministry for dealing with enlistment skilled men War Office has given orders for Hargreaves to be returned to civil life and therefore stoppage of work cannot be justified or permitted. Grievances as to enlistment of skilled men are being examined and dealt with in consultation with the trade union concerned who are assisting to maintain output of munitions essential at this time of national crisis. No stoppage of work on munitions must take place.

Munissuply, London.

Twenty minutes earlier a telegram had been received from Hargreaves himself saying that he had heard nothing about release. This confirmed the warnings which the shop stewards committee had given to the men concerning possible promises from the authorities. But a further precaution had been taken to check any government tricks. Two men had been sent to the camp where Hargreaves was stationed and no confirmatory word about release had been received from them.

The mass meeting of the men promptly intimated to the Government that 'Hargreaves must be present in Sheffield before the men will agree to return to work.'

Meanwhile the delegates who had been sent to the various engineering centres were doing their work effectively. The methods adopted struck the imagination of the workers everywhere. The grievances of the Sheffield men found support wherever the delegates appeared. The week-end saw big developments. A whole series of mass meetings was arranged. The Barrow engineers were very prompt to answer because they had already developed a system of shop stewards. They held a mass meeting on the second day of the strike and pledged themselves to join in within twenty-four hours.

The third day of the strike saw the capitulation of the Government in fact as well as word. Hargreaves was released and the two delegates of the shop stewards waiting at the camp escorted him back to Sheffield. The day following the appearance of Hargreaves before a mass meeting of the men the return to work was conducted in a well organized manner. There was no scramble back to the workshops immediately it was rumoured that the strike was won. The men waited for the mass meeting and its decision.

The enthusiasm engendered by this victory was very great. As in the case of the Labour Withholding Committee of Glasgow, action and victory raised the prestige of the shop stewards enormously. For the time being the shop stewards committee became the dominant authority. The men felt that it was only through this new form of organization that the unions could now justify themselves in the least as defenders of the interests of the workers.

Much anti-war propaganda was fearlessly conducted at the meetings. The attack upon the engineering workers was described as part of the universal attempt of capitalism to hold the workers in subjection. The war was denounced as an imperialist war for robbing the workers and not a war for their liberation.

The action of the Barrow engineers who had come out on strike in support on the third day of the strike helped a great deal to demonstrate that factory organization was a more powerful instrument than the workers had seen hitherto. It reached all the workers in the quickest possible time and facilitated the rapid mobilization of forces for action.

Early in January of 1917 another great mass meeting was organized by the Sheffield shop stewards for the rendering of an account and meeting all the obligations arising out of the November dispute and to consider the next steps to be taken in the development of the movement. The meeting was composed of skilled and semi-skilled workers. It says much for the prestige of the shop stewards at this time that they were able to get a unanimous decision from the meeting in favour of extending the organization to include all the workers in the factories, skilled, semi-skilled and unskilled workers, men and women.

The proposals were, that in every workshop there should be a workshop committee composed of delegates elected by all the workers in the shop. Wherever possible, and this was possible in most cases, any worker elected as a shop steward should receive the endorsement of his union. But those who were not members of a union were not prohibited from election to the workshop committees if they had the confidence of the workers in the shop. This of course led to much recruiting of workers into the various unions.

In every factory it was proposed that there should be a factory committee made up of representatives of each workshop committee. All the shop stewards of the factories were to be united in the Sheffield Engineering Workers' Committee.

This was visualized as a part of a national industrial organization rising up, not in antagonism to the unions but to the existing leadership and form of organization. It was considered as a means of re-organizing the working class movement on the basis of industrial unionism. As in the case of the Clyde Workers' Committee the revolutionary workers were taking the lead and the influence of their ideas on the course of events is clear.

But the Clyde Movement was now subdued and broken. They did not render any assistance to the Sheffield strike nor to any other of the strikes that followed in quick succession during the war period.

CHAPTER VII

A SERIES OF STRIKES

On March 21st, 1917, six thousand engineers of Barrow-in-Furness 'downed tools'. This was a protest strike against the systematic cutting of rates established under the Premium Bonus system. Under this method of payment, a man is given a job and the time taken to do it is estimated by an individual known as the rate fixer. Suppose that it is estimated by him that a job can be done in twelve hours. According to the agreement between the employer and the workmen this estimated time must then be increased fifty per cent to form what is known as the base time. In the example mentioned the base time would be eighteen hours. If then the worker did the job in twelve hours he would receive fifteen hours pay for it, thus receiving as bonus fifty per cent of the difference between the base time and the actual time taken to do the job.

It was the rule, that once the base time has been fixed on a job it should not be altered unless it was challenged by the worker as inadequate. But the employers were not satisfied. They began to force the pace and to cut the base rates. It happened also that the rate fixer was an objectionable individual in his dealings with the men. The result was that the men would not stand for the reductions or tolerate the rate fixer. Hence the strike.

The shop stewards were well organized, although their organization was confined to skilled workers. It was under their leadership that the men took action. The men put forward demands for the abolition of the premium bonus system and the institution of a flat rate of wages equal to time and a half of the present rate, and the dismissal of the rate fixer.

The efforts to secure a resumption of work by the executive committees of the various unions met with failure. Meanwhile the shop stewards endeavoured to secure support from other engineering towns. As yet there was no such thing as a national leadership of the shop stewards. Delegates were sent to the Clyde, Sheffield and Manchester. The Barrow men looked specially to Sheffield because of the prompt way in which the Barrow men had responded to the call of the Sheffield engineers a few months previously.

The issue of the strike however complicated matters. The premium bonus system did not operate in Sheffield where a totally different piece work system prevailed. A wide campaign had to be initiated to explain the issue in opposition to an official union campaign to prevent the extension of the strike.

The strike had been on for ten days before the Sheffield shop stewards succeeded in getting a decision for sympathetic strike action. Before this decision could be put into operation the Barrow engineers came to terms.

This experience had the effect of raising the question of the national organization of the shop stewards. A conference was held in Manchester on May 5th and 6th under the leadership of Arthur MacManus, who, after deportation from the Clyde, had gone with several other of the deportees to Liverpool. But this conference was not a very representative gathering and before it could take further steps the whole movement in the engineering industry in England was involved in a great dispute.

A strike started in Rochdale at the firm of Tweedale and Smalley's. There had been an attempt on the part of the employers to extend 'dilution' of labour to commercial work as distinct from war work. The workers felt convinced that even on war work the employers were exploiting the war situation for their own profitable ends and regarded the talk of the Government and the trade union officials about the 'control of profits' as so much idle chatter. When, therefore, they were faced with the extension of dilution to commercial work the skilled workers felt this to be the last straw.

There had been a ballot on the question inside the unions of the skilled workers. The Executive of the A.S.E. was the only executive of these unions which did not recommend the acceptance of the scheme. The ballot vote was overwhelmingly against the scheme. The effort of Messrs. Tweedale and Smalley was an attempt to apply the terms in spite of the adverse vote.

A further aggravating feature of the situation was the abolition of what was known as the 'Trade Card Scheme'. This scheme was part of the price paid by the Government to the skilled unions to secure their acceptance of 'dilution' on war work. It ensured the retention of the skilled workers in industry. The unions of the skilled workers issued cards to their members which served as exemption cards over-ruling the calling-up notice of the military authorities. It was regarded as a certificate of indispensability of the holders because of their engagement on war work.

It was now proposed to abandon this scheme and place the responsibility for exemption of all workers entirely in the hands of the military tribunals operating in consultation with the employers. This was regarded as the completion of the process of industrial and military conscription which the Government had had in view from the beginning of the war. The masses of the workers were against conscription in all its forms. At the Labour Party Conference in 1916, 1,998,000 voted against conscription compared with 783,000 in favour. But three months later a second conference turned down conscription by 1,796,000 to 219,000. With such a large opposition the Government had to manœuvre to achieve its ends by other means than that of the direct introduction of conscription. The abolition of the trade card scheme was the completion of the manœuvre and meant the handing over of all power to the military authorities.

The feeling roused by these questions was exceedingly keen. So much was this the case that the local officials of the unions lined up with the shop stewards' committees in favour of active opposition.

Immediately after the Manchester Conference the strike spread throughout the engineering workshops of Manchester and Sheffield. The resolutions adopted at the strike meetings demanded the abolition of dilution on private work and the reinstatement of the trade card scheme.

The strike spread in all directions. Each day saw some new district joining the strikers, Coventry, Birmingham, London, Woolwich, Leicester, Rugby, Derby, Liverpool, Birkenhead, Leeds, Newcastle. But the Clyde did not join in. The strike in England spread until some two hundred and fifty thousand engineering workers were on the streets.

During the strike Messrs. Tweedale and Smalleys were

brought before the Munitions Tribunal for the violation of the Munitions Act. They were fined £35 and twenty guineas costs. The situation had developed too far however for such a trivial punishment to do other than incense the men. At the same time the Government proceeded with the 'Dilution Bill' which snatched away all the concessions made to the unions at the beginning of the war.

On May 15th, 1917, a national conference of delegates from the strike committees was held in London. The Conference sat three days. Its statements were suppressed by the censor despite the protests of W. C. Anderson, M.P., in the House of Commons. The Conference asked the Minister of Munitions to meet a deputation from the Conference. Dr. Addison, the then Minister of Munitions replied that he would only meet such a deputation if asked by the trade union executives and accompanied by them.

The Government proceeded with the Dilution Bill. W. C. Anderson moved the adjournment of the House of Commons and attacked the Government but was defeated without a division. The trade union executives basking in the congratulations of the Government for their war services, supported the Government. But the strike continued.

Then the Government took drastic action. In the early hours of May 18th seven strike leaders were arrested and warrants issued for three others. The conference, which was held in the Socialist Hall, Walworth, was raided and correspondence and reports were seized by the police. The names of the arrested men were G. Peet, Keeley, Burgess, Hill, MacManus, Dingley and Cassidy. Later Watson also was arrested.

These actions of the Government changed the situation entirely. All attention was diverted from the issues which had caused the strike and concentrated upon the demand for the release of the arrested men. The shop stewards surrendered their independence and called on the assistance of the A.S.E. executive and a deputation of the stewards, led by J. T. Brownlie and W. Hutchinson, met the Minister of Munitions.

This delegation arrived at an agreement with the Minister of Munitions which amounted to the complete capitulation of the Shop Stewards' Conference, both to the Government and the Union Executive. It recommended that the men should resume work at once on the following terms: the arrested men to be released at once on their own recognisance; no further arrests to be made; the unofficial leaders of the strikers to leave further negotiations with the Government regarding existing differences to the trade union officials.

On May 19th the Shop Stewards' Conference endorsed the agreement and the A.S.E. Executive issued instructions that work should be resumed. But only sections of the workers returned to work. The Barrow engineers who had not entered the strike at the beginning now decided to strike. Burgess and Hill from Sheffield had been released on bail, but the Sheffield workers refused to return to work in spite of their appeals. The men were angry with what they regarded as the complete capitulation of the Shop Stewards' Conference in face of Government intimidation.

In the meantime the Government felt, and rightly so, that it had got control of the situation. With the aid of the lawyers they secured a statement from the eight arrested men which said:

'I undertake to adhere to the agreement arrived at on Saturday, May 19th, 1917, between the Ministry of Munitions and the Executive Committee of the A.S.E. acting at the request of the unofficial strike committee and on their behalf.'

The Government dropped the charges. But it was not until May 24th that the workers of Sheffield, Barrow, Manchester and Liverpool returned to work. The districts which had well-organized shop stewards' committees proved their capacity to hold firmly to their purpose but were forced to retreat in face of the collapse of the strike in those centres where the strike committees had had to be improvised at the last moment.

This was a sad ending to a great strike. Its defeat was due primarily to the absence of a firmly established leadership and organization guided by a definite policy. A spontaneous strike without inner organization capable of promptly giving it direction and leadership when the action is on so large a scale, is doomed to defeat before it begins. The idea that a spontaneous movement of the masses will 'spontaneously throw up' a leadership and a policy is moonshine. Leaders who come to the front in hours of crisis have invariably years of preparation behind them however obscure it may be. This strike had not been prepared. The Manchester conference was called for an entirely different purpose than that of beginning a strike. It is doubtful whether any of the leaders anticipated so great a development of mass action. There is no record of such anticipation either at the conference or in the subsequent discussions of the strike. It was the least planned of any of the strikes led by the shop stewards and having no plan or policy other than that of extending the strike against dilution, the leaders were overwhelmed by the situation the strike had created immediately the Government acted decisively against them.

Within a few months a strike broke out at Coventry which caught the movement by surprise. Ever since the May strike the shop stewards' movement in Coventry had forged ahead in close co-operation with the local union machinery. A Joint Engineering Board of the Engineering Unions had been in existence for some years. The shop stewards practically took charge of this body. The employers decided to fight it and refused to recognize its authority.

The shop stewards led the men out on strike, but the National Administrative Council of the Shop Stewards, which had been established after the May strike, knew nothing whatever about it. Before the slow moving machinery could be got to work and other districts aroused to what was taking place, the Coventry shop stewards had accepted negotiations and returned to work.

But the employers and the trade union executives did not let the matter drop with the termination of the strike. It was obvious to them that unless they could bring this movement completely under their control the time would soon arrive when the authority of the union leaders would be lost.

Earlier in the year, on March 17th, the Government had issued what became known as the 'Whitley Report'. This report had followed upon an examination of the 'causes of unrest' in industry. It aimed at killing the workshop movement as an independent movement, by retaining the form of organization and changing its principles from class war to class collaboration. It proposed that there should be workshop committees and works committees, but these should have on them representatives of the employers as well as the workers. They were called 'joint committees of employers and workers'.

On November 10th, 1917, there was held a national conference of employers and trade union representatives for the purpose of furthering these proposals. The shop stewards therefore were faced with a new form of opposition more dangerous than the challenges of the Government. The National Committee of the shop stewards had convened a national conference of the shop stewards in Manchester on the same date as the employers' conference. This conference refused to have anything to do with Whitleyism and began a campaign against it.

On March 7th, 1918, the whole of the workers at the Vulcan Motor Works, Southport, engaged at that time on munition work, struck work to secure the re-instatement of the writer of this book. He was unjustly accused of being a 'bad' timekeeper, but actually the manager had discovered he was employing 'an agitator' and was anxious to be rid of him. The solidarity of the strike was extraordinary. Men, women, girls and apprentices acted in unison. The strike lasted two weeks without weakening in the least and the management was compelled to climb down and effect the re-instatement demanded by the workers.

A further large strike took place in Birmingham in the autumn of the same year. This was known as the 'embargo strike'. It had its origin in what was known as the 'embargo scheme' of the Government which forbad the employment of new skilled workmen by any firm without a special licence from the Ministry of Munitions. The purpose of the measure was to facilitate the transfer of semi-skilled and unskilled workers to skilled workers' jobs at lower rates of pay.

The strike began at the Austin Motor Factory and rapidly spread through the engineering factories of Birmingham and Coventry. The strike lasted ten days and whilst it appeared that the Government was able to negotiate terms, the strike killed the scheme and little more was heard of it.

This was the last of the strikes carried through by the shop stewards during the war. Once more it proved to be a localized strike and the national organization was not brought into action. There are important reasons for this which it will be necessary to examine.

CHAPTER VIII

THE INFLUENCE OF THE RUSSIAN REVOLUTION

THE whole history of the shop stewards is the history of a strike wave developing in the engineering centres. It was a revolt against the new conditions imposed by the dilution of Labour which were breaking down the strongholds of the skilled workers. This strike movement was harnessed by the revolutionary socialists of the S.L.P., the B.S.P. and the syndicalists. It was quite natural therefore that national organization should follow in the wake of the strikes rather than precede them.

The first attempt to develop national organization and leadership, as already mentioned, was the calling of a conference of 'Workers' Committees' on the initiative of MacManus and the other deportees. The Conference was held in Hyndman Hall, Manchester, on November 5th and 6th, 1916. There were present representatives from the Clyde workers' committee, Barrow, Manchester, London, and Birkenhead. It should be understood however that these workers' committees were not representative shop steward committees. They were propaganda groups composed of individual shop stewards. This conference issued a manifesto stating that,

> 'Our purpose must not be misconstrued. We are out for unity and closer organization of all trades in the industry – one union being our ultimate goal.
> We will support the officials just so long as they rightly

> represent the workers, but we will act independently immediately they misrepresent them.
>
> Being composed of delegates from every shop, and untrammelled by obsolete rules or law, we claim to represent the true feelings of the workers. We can act according to the merits of the case and the desire of the rank and file.'

The object of the workers' committees was defined as follows:

> 'The furtherance of the interests of working-class organizations as a partisan effort to improve the position of Labour in the present and to ultimately assist in the abolition of the wages system.'

It had no programme apart from these brief statements of a general character. It did not define its attitude to political parties. This is not peculiar to this conference in that the shop stewards' movement throughout its existence never discussed the question until in its closing days, after the formation of the Communist Party in 1920. In this it was really carrying on the traditions of the syndicalist conferences. At the same time it shows how little the revolutionary socialists of this time understood the role of a revolutionary party.

Although the leading shop stewards were also leaders of the S.L.P. and the B.S.P. the parties did not discuss their responsibilities for directing the movement.

The conference set up a national committee under the chairmanship of A. MacManus with S. Bradley as secretary. This committee was soon merged into the more representative conference of May 5th and 6th, 1917, which became embroiled in the extension of the strike begun at Rochdale. Hence it was not until August 18th and 19th of 1917 that a fully representative national conference of shop stewards was organized. It was held in the Milton Hall, Manchester. There were delegates present representing the shop stewards committees of Barrow, Bolton, Bradford, Bristol, Chatham, Coventry, Crayford, Dalmuir, Elswick, and Scotswood (Newcastle), Halifax, Invergordon, Leigh, Leeds, Liverpool, Manchester, Newton-le-Willows, Salford, Stockport, Clyde Workers' Committee, Sheffield Workers' Committee, Iron Moulders' Committee of Scotland and London Workers' Committee.

In all but a few cases the shop stewards' committees here represented were confined to the skilled workers. In some cases they included semi-skilled workers and in fewer cases extended to the unskilled workers and women workers. There were no women present at the conference.

MacManus was the chairman of the conference and at once brought into it the influence of the great Workers' and Soldiers' Council Convention which had been held in Leeds only a few weeks previously. This convention revealed how great had been the response of the British working class to the Russian Revolution of March, 1917. In it the pent up feeling against the war found expression. 1,150 delegates came to the Convention from all over Britain. It was called on the initiative of the Independent Labour Party and the B.S.P. who had formed a united socialist council for the purpose and appealed to the British workers to follow the example of Russia. MacDonald and Snowden, who were then leaders of the I.L.P., played a leading role in the convention and supported resolutions, the like of which had never been seen in the history of the British working-class movement.

Mr. MacDonald moved the following resolution: –

'This Conference of Labour and Socialist and Democratic organizations of Britain, hails the Russian Revolution. With gratitude and admiration it congratulates the Russian people upon the Revolution which has overthrown a tyranny that resisted the intellectual and social development of Russia, which has removed the standing menace to aggressive imperialism in Eastern Europe, and which has liberated the people of Russia for the great work of establishing political and economic freedom on a firm foundation and of taking the foremost part in the international movement for *working-class emancipation* from all forms of political, economic and imperialist oppression and exploitation.'

He said, 'I think there will be no minority upon this resolution. It is fashionable in some quarters in this country to say, "We congratulate the Russians upon their revolution, but in some respects we regret it." To-day we congratulate the Russians on the revolution without reservations whatever. We do it not because we are compelled to be glad but because we wanted it to happen . . . The Revolution did not come in a night. Never has precious harvest been sown with more precious seed. The best of the women of Russia, the young women and the young men, laying down their lives that liberty might be advanced in their native land. All that story of oppression, all that long toll of martyrdom, is drawn like a trail of blood across the history of Russia, at last bursting out into a great flood of light and hope, not only for Russia, thank God, but for the whole world.

'Our congratulations are absolutely unstinted and unqualified. And what has it done for Russia itself? The moment the Revolution came the gates of the prisons were unbarred, censorship was abolished, and the light of reason allowed to play for the first time upon the problems of the world . . .

'The old Russian Government was a sink of corruption. It was the most corrupt of all the governments of Europe. St. Petersburg was the nursery of the worst forms of diplomacy, the garden where the worst traditions of diplomacy were carefully watered and nurtured. All was restless. All was untrustworthy, all was unsafe, all was criminal.

'When the war broke out organized labour in this country lost the initiative. It became a mere echo of the *old governing classes opinion.* Now the Russian Revolution has once again given you the chance to take the initiative yourselves. Let us lay down our terms, make our own diplomacy, see to it that we have our own international meetings. . .'[1]

After MacDonald came W. C. Anderson, M.P., with the remarkable resolution proposing the formation of 'Workers' and Soldiers' Councils'.[2] In the course of his speech he said, 'If we are going to have justice for the soldiers, for

[1] *The Herald*, June 3rd, 1917.

[2] 'This conference calls upon the constituent bodies at once to establish in every town, urban and rural district, Councils of Workmen and Soldiers' Delegates for initiating and co-ordinating working-class activity in support of the policy set out in the foregoing resolutions and to work strenuously for a peace made by the peoples of the various countries, and for the complete political and economic emancipation of international labour. Such councils shall also watch diligently for and resist every encroachment upon civil liberty; shall give special attention to the position of women employed in industry and generally support the work of the

the wives and the widows and the children of soldiers, and if we are going to have industrial freedom for the workers, the workman and the soldier must join hands.

' "Ah," they say, "This is revolution." If a revolution be the conquest of political power by an hitherto disinherited class, if revolution be that we are not going to put up in the future with what we have put up with in the past, we are not going to have the chains and the poverty of the past, then the sooner we have a revolution in this country the better . . . .' 'We are building up, taking the first steps to set up the necessary machinery for dealing with the complete emancipation of international labour.'

Mr. Robert Williams in seconding the resolution said, 'The resolution, if it means anything at all, means that which is contained in the oft used phrase from socialist platforms – The dictatorship of the Proletariat.'

Mr. Phillip Snowden (now Lord Snowden) drew the attention of the conference to the telegram from the Russian Workmen's and Soldiers' Councils and said it had been agreed to send the following reply: 'The largest and greatest Convention of Labour, socialist and democratic bodies held in Great Britain during this generation has to-day approved Russia's declaration of foreign policy and war aims, and has pledged itself to *work through its newly constituted Workmen's and Soldiers' Council* for an immediate democratic peace. The Convention received

trade unions; shall take active steps to stop the exploitation of food and all the necessaries of life, and shall concern themselves with questions affecting the pensions of wounded and disabled soldiers and the maintenance grants payable to the dependents of men serving in the army and navy and the making of adequate provision for the training of disabled soldiers and for suitable and remunerative work for the men on their return to civil life. And further, that the conveners of this conference be appointed a provisional committee, whose duty shall be to assist the formation of Workmen's and Soldiers' Councils and generally give effect to the policy determined by the conference.' – *The Herald*, June 3rd, 1917.

your telegram of congratulation with gratitude and enthusiasm.'

The first impact of the Russian Revolution carried the working-class movement of this country much further than the leaders wanted to go. This was soon proved by the way in which the leaders ignored the instructions of the convention and allowed the movement to die down. But in spite of this it had demonstrated that revolutionary thought and feeling was much further advanced than either the labour leaders or the Government had thought. It had done more. It showed the grouping of working-class organization into Trades Councils and Labour Parties had a class significance that marked them out once more as the means for the concentration of working-class forces for common action. There were 209 Trades Councils and Local Labour Party delegates present and upon these bodies would fall the task of gathering the forces together to make the Workers' and Soldiers' Councils, if they were formed.

The leaders, however, realized that they had acted dangerously and began to retreat. So long as they could echo the congratulations of Government politicians to the Russian Revolution, which at this time they thought would stop and consolidate as a capitalist revolution, they felt themselves in good and safe company. But the moment they realized that they were unleashing the forces of proletarian revolution the tune changed. As soon as the workers carried through the Proletarian Revolution in November, 1917, the very leaders who at the Leeds Convention, proposed and supported the proposition for Workers' and Soldiers' Councils in Britain, became definitely counter-revolutionary in their speeches and writings.

When the shop stewards' conference met, however, the

full influence of the Leeds Convention was still felt. The chairman and several delegates spoke of the imminence of revolutionary developments in Europe and the growing feeling against the war in Britain itself. But the effect on the conference decisions was regrettable.

The features of the Russian Revolution which appeared to the delegates and especially the leaders as the most obvious were the mass uprisings and the formation of soviets. No one present had any knowledge whatever of the history of the Russian working-class movement, its party struggles or its leaders, whilst their own political theories, as already shown, favoured mass action, spontaneous movements of the masses, and opposition to centralized leadership.

They saw the significance of the workshop movement and at once felt their kinship with the soviets. But what they saw also retarded all efforts to secure a centralized leadership, and strengthened them in the 'rank and file' philosophy of the 'Miners' Next Step'. This was evident when the conference discussed the question of electing a national committee. J. Henderson, representing the Clyde workers' committee, moved 'that we do not form a national committee', on the grounds that a number of delegates had 'not received a mandate'. This was seconded by J. B. Watson representing the Dalmuir shop stewards. Another proposed that it should only be a provisional committee. Another that it should 'represent every district by each district being represented on it'. Finally, G. Peet set the conference at its ease by assuring it that the national committee[1] would be 'an administrative committee' and not an executive committee and all matters would be referred

[1] The first National Committee elected at this conference consisted of A. MacManus, Chairman; D. Peet, Sec.; J. T. Murphy, Ass. Sec.; T. Hurst, W. Gallacher, S. Bradley, T. Dingley, and H. King.

to the rank and file. This was confirmed by the perambulating title of the national committee, which was 'The National Administrative Council of the Shop Stewards and Workers' Committees'. Thus the first national committee was formed, but held theories which prevented it from giving the leadership which the movement needed more than at any time since its formation.

On October 14th and 15th, 1917, another important conference was held which helped to swell the ranks of the shop stewards' movement. This was the conference of the National Metal, Engineering and Shipbuilding Amalgamation Committees held in Newcastle. There were 150 delegates present from all parts of the country. The leaders of the conference were W. F. Watson and P. G. Keeley. The declared object of these committees since their formation in 1909 had been the amalgamation of all the unions in the engineering and shipbuilding industry into one union for the whole industry.

To a large extent these committees had been eclipsed by the shop stewards' and workers' committees. Many of them had been transformed into the latter. Several of the leaders of the amalgamation committees, however, thought the time had come to use both these movements as the means to start a new industrial union. The two leaders named were the principals in this move. They had come to this conference with the determination to put the question to the test. Their proposal was 'to give the union executives a final chance to amalgamate. Should they refuse to take action, we shall immediately form ourselves into an Engineering and Shipbuilding Workers' Industrial Union'.

The shop stewards had already turned down such a proposal and came forward at this conference with a counter proposal for the fusion of the amalgamation committees with the workers' committees. This resolution was carried by a large majority. Thus ended in defeat a dangerous move which would, had it been carried through, have added one more union to the already chaotic union position in the industry.

Quickly following this decision a joint conference of the shop stewards and the amalgamation committees was held. It met on January 5th and 6th, 1918, and elected a new national council including some of the leading men of the amalgamation committees.[1]

This conference proceeded at once to define the attitude of the shop stewards to the Bolshevik Revolution of November, 1917. It declared enthusiastically its solidarity with the revolution and pledged the movement to do all in its power to support it. It demanded that 'the Government should at once accept the invitation of the Soviet Government to consider peace terms' and endorsed the line taken by the bolsheviks.

In these decisions the conference was undoubtedly expressing the feelings of the great mass of the workers as was shown by the tremendous reception given to Litvinoff at the Labour Party Conference held at Nottingham in the same month. The influence of the Russian Revolution on the working class roused great masses of workers against the continuation of the war. The same conference that welcomed Litvinoff also recorded a minority vote of 720,000 in favour of the Labour Party representatives withdrawing from the Coalition Government and forbidding Labour members from joining any future capitalist government.

[1] The new Council consisted of A. MacManus, D. Peet, J. T. Murphy, F. Smith, W. F. Watson, J. Tanner, F. Delaney, J. Finigan, T. Hurst, P. G. Keeley.

The shop stewards' conference had to discuss what was to be done to oppose the *new* 'Man Power' proposals embodied in a further military service measure before the House of Commons. The demand for men for the front was leading to what was called 'a comb out' of the factories. It was decided to wage a campaign against the proposals and to test the feeling of the workers in the factories on the question of their preparedness to take strike action to stop the war.

When the National Council of the Shop Stewards met a month later, the new military offensive of the Western front had quietened a great deal of the opposition to the Government's proposals. Nevertheless some interesting facts were brought to light. W. F. Watson reported that 'one hundred thousand workers in London were ready to strike against the war'. This turned out to be the 'opinion of some comrades on the London committee because no attempt to test the opinions of the workers in the factories had been made'. The Clyde workers' committee instructed its delegate to vote for strike action, but when asked by the council as to what had been done to ensure support he reported that a workshop vote had been conducted amongst the A.S.E. members, 8,500 of whom had voted for the re-introduction of the trade card scheme and 8,000 against. The opinion of the Manchester and Sheffield workers were tested by workshop meetings and were opposed to strike action against the war. The committee were therefore unable to give any strike call. The tremendous battles taking place in France at the time of the workshop meetings certainly gave a set-back to the wave of anti-war feeling that was manifest at the beginning of the year.

The council then initiated a grandiose scheme for

mobilizing the whole working class through the joint effort of the workshop committees, the trade unions, trades councils and labour parties, on the basis of a democratic programme, of 'peace without annexations and indemnities', and in favour of Labour taking a decisive part in the making of the peace. Although this scheme was discussed at a subsequent conference held in March at which for the first time appeared representatives from the miners' reform committees and the railwaymen's vigilance committees, little came of it.

This conference, held in Sheffield, quickly passed to the discussion of organizational questions. On this occasion a struggle ensued between the engineering delegates and the delegates of the miners and railwaymen on the possibility of applying the principles of workshop organization to the mines and railways. Both the miners' reform committees and the railwaymen's vigilance committees were organized as groups within the trade union branches. Their representatives argued that they could change the structure and the leadership of their unions through the ordinary machinery of the unions and therefore there was no need to organize in any other way than as reform and vigilance committees inside the union branches.

The shop stewards insisted that the lodge and branch representation was not enough. They argued that it was only a comparatively small section of the workers who attended the trade union branches. To be effective in controlling the conditions of labour and certainly to achieve their object of controlling industry, the workers must be organized on the job. So long as the railwaymen were unorganized in the goods yards, the railway workshops, railway stations, engine sheds and all the other units of industrial activity, they could not hope to be effective.

Whilst it was admitted that the miners' lodge approximated more closely in its composition to particular pits the shop stewards refused to accept the idea that pit committees were unnecessary. The lodges met infrequently. They were not organized to control any job. The pit committees on the contrary functioned on the job every day and were thus capable of prompt action in the defence of the miners' interests.

It was not a difficult matter to expose the incapacity of the trade unions to control industry. It was also easy to question their democracy. Some unions have no branch meetings at all. Others meet once a quarter, others once a month or once a fortnight. The attendance at branch meetings is small. An examination of the voting of the unions on major questions will show that it is only on very rare occasions that the majority of the members can be mobilized to vote and that there are very few officials who hold office on more than a fifteen per cent vote and many who hold it on less.[1]

[1] Record of some recent Trade Union voting (prepared by the Labour Research Department, 1919).

Engineering Industry.

Amalgamated Society of Engineers. Membership 297,000.

			Total vote	*Percentage*
47 Hour Week	For	36,397		
	Against	27,684	64,081	21
Chairman of Executive (Second Ballot)				
	Winner	24,522		
	Loser	13,294	37,816	11
Affiliation to Trades Union Congress				
	For	28,304		
	Against	5,812	34,116	10
Scheme of Amalgamation				
	For	30,478		
	Against	2,958	33,436	10
Man Power proposals (Postal Ballot)				
	For	27,416		
(A record vote.)	Against	120,675	148,091	50

Of course it would be wrong to assume that the voting is the exact measure of the authority wielded by the leadership of the unions. Their authority extends not only to the whole membership of the unions but to large sections of the workers who are not members of the unions.

The discussion on this occasion ended in deadlock, but by 1919 and 1920 all sections of the trade union movement were talking in terms of workshop organization and 'part control of industry', 'encroaching control' and 'complete control of industry'. Even Mr. Sidney Webb discovered a place for 'the producers organizations' in his schematic outlines of the future of capitalist society.

			Total vote	*Percentage*
Boilermakers' Society. Membership 80,000.				
47 Hour Week	For	3,974		
	Against	9,948	13,822	17
On Demarcation Scheme	For	1,952		
	Against	226	2,178	2.5
Patternmakers' Society. Membership 10,500.				
47 Hour Week	For	2,267		
	Against	2,151	4,418	45
Affiliation to Labour Party	For	1,649		
	Against	249	1,899	18
Carpenters, Cabinet-makers and Joiners. Membership 125,000.				
47 Hour Week	For	17,180		
	Against	7,151	24,331	19
Election of Assistant Secretary				
	Winner	13,093		
	Loser	478	13,571	10
Furnishing Trades' Association. 16,000 membership.				
47 Hour Week	For	2,907		
	Against	269	3,176	19
Man Power Proposals	For	794		
	Against	1,066	1,960	12
Workers' Union. Membership 350,000 approx.				
47 Hour Week	For	35,486		
	Against	3,624	39,110	11

The practice of taking ballot votes is nearly confined to building, engineering, and textile unions, some clothing unions and boot and shoe operatives. Others take decisions by delegate meeting.

It is significant however that in all these discussions the central question of the CONQUEST OF POLITICAL POWER by the working class was entirely overlooked. The shop stewards did not discuss it. Had this question been clearly understood then a totally different attitude would have developed on the question of union organization and 'the control of industry'. It would have been realized that the unions will never be reorganized to control industry until the working class has conquered political power. Every step in the direction of industrial unionism is of value to the extent that it facilitates the massing of the workers for common action in defence of their economic conditions against the increasing pressure and exploitation of the capitalists, but 'workers control of industry' without 'workers ownership of industry' is utterly impossible. The change of ownership is a political question, indeed the outstanding political question of our time, involving a complete and fundamental change in the relation of classes.

This question is the key question of Bolshevism and Fascism. The Bolshevik Revolution in Russia settled the question of ownership for the working class and led to the reorganization of the trade unions in terms of industrial unionism. The Fascist counter-revolutions of Italy and Germany represent the violent, desperate, class resistance of the defenders of private property and capitalist relations in society. They have brought with them the destruction of the trade unions and reorganization of the workers as industrial helots.

But the shop stewards and the revolutionaries generally did not appreciate what Marx had set forth in the 'Communist Manifesto' of 1847. They were immersed in the daily life of the factories and impressed with the power that the industrial revolution of the war period had thrust upon them. They were engrossed in the job of organizing women into the unions, breaking down the barriers between skilled and unskilled workers, fighting against every encroachment the war machine of British capitalism made upon the workers 'at the point of production'. They felt that if only the methods they had adopted were taken up and applied by the whole working-class movement then the victory of the working class over the capitalists was not far off. Not until the war was over and the employers swept the workers into the streets by hundreds of thousands were their illusions destroyed and 'encroaching control' lost its appeal.

When first the shop stewards' movement became a movement on a national scale however, it appeared as if the theories of the industrial unionists as expressed by Connolly were finding their fulfilment. A militant spirit began to spread throughout the working-class movement and all eyes were turned upon this new phenomenon. When suddenly, the Russian Revolution made everybody talk of 'Workers' and Soldiers' Councils' there were many besides the shop stewards, who saw the new workshop movement as the forerunner of Workers' and Soldiers' Councils in Britain. The absence of unemployment gave added strength and confidence to all sections of the working-class movement. The trade unions grew enormously. The Labour Party, whilst growing by leaps and bounds was caught by the revolutionary sentiments and impulses that were stirring the mass of the working class. In fact it was the pressure of the masses that forced the open break with the Coalition Government in 1918, and commenced the most far-reaching changes yet made in the history of the British Labour Movement.

CHAPTER IX

LABOUR LEADERS AND THE WAR

ALREADY during the year 1917, especially after the Workers' Council Convention and the great engineers' strike, it was clear to the Government and the leaders of the Labour Party, that new problems were confronting them. There could be no going back to pre-war conditions. The industrial revolution of the war was accompanied by social changes which altered the outlook of the masses. The workers had seen millions upon millions of pounds pouring into the pockets of war profiteers while the best of the young manhood of the nation was destroyed in useless slaughter on the battlefields of Europe. They had seen millions of pounds literally thrown away by the Government whilst their daily bread deteriorated and they were being called upon to make extraordinary efforts. Military and industrial conscription had become facts of their daily life.

The effect of the Russian Revolution, just as the surging strike movement was reaching its peak, was immense. To the Russian working class and peasantry and the war-weary millions of ill-equipped soldiers, this revolution was the way out of the holocaust. To the British working class it was the lightning flash of a gathering storm, an indication not only that the war must soon end, but that the faith of millions of people in the durability of capitalism was shaken.

The Government answered this new situation by initiating a great propaganda concerning 'Reconstruction after the War'. Wonderful schemes were put on paper. 'Reconstruction Conferences' were organized. 'Homes fit for heroes to dwell in', were promised. 'Limehousing' on the grand scale replaced the accusations of slackness and drunkenness levelled against the workers. 'Whitleyism' in industry replaced the direct repression of independent working-class action.

The Labour Party and trade union leaders were in a more difficult position than the Government. They were just as anxious to circumvent the revolutionary aspirations of the workers, but their power depended upon the confidence and support of this class. They had therefore the difficult task of making concessions to socialism and at the same time subordinating the movement as a whole to the principal aim of the war, the defeat of Germany. How effectively they carried this policy into international politics is a matter of history recorded by their own spokesman, Mr. Sidney Webb. 'From the first,' he says, 'it was seen to be important to get the representatives of the trade unions and socialist organizations of the allied nations, and not merely their Governments, united in a declaration of the aims and the *justification of a war that was everywhere outraging working-class idealism.*[1]

What a declaration! In August, 1914, they denounced the war as *unjustifiable!*

In February, 1915, they organized in London a conference of working-class organizations of France, Belgium, Great Britain and Russia with a view to a 'justification of a war that was everywhere outraging working-class idealism'. The Bolsheviks were not invited. Litvinoff

[1] *History of Trade Unionism*, p. 693.

attended and tried to read a declaration, but was prevented from doing so by the chairman.[1]

In the spring of 1916, the Secretary of the Labour Party, Mr. Henderson, was party to, as a member of the Asquith Cabinet, the crushing of the Irish Rebellion and the judicial murder of James Connolly, the Irish socialist. Both the Labour Party and the I.L.P. denounced the rebellion.

'Later on,' says Mr. Webb, 'when a Minority Party had been formed among the German Socialists, and when the Austrian and Hungarian working-class movements were also in revolt against the militarism of their Governments, repeated efforts were made by the Labour Party to encourage this revolt, and for this purpose to obtain the necessary Government facilities for a meeting in some neutral city, of the working-class 'International', *at which the Allied case could be laid* before the neutrals, and a basis found for united action with all working-

[1] The Declaration of the Russian Social Democratic Party (Bolshevik) to the London Conference. . . .

The statement first of all reproaches the International Socialist Bureau for not sending an invitation to the Party to be present. It then proceeds to denounce the aims of the conference and to put forward the following demands:

1. That Vandervelde, Guesde, and Sembat immediately quit the bourgeois cabinets of Belgium and France;
2. That the Belgian and French socialist parties sever the so-called 'national bloc' which is a renunciation of the socialist banner, and serves to cover up the orgies of chauvinism indulged in by the bourgeoisie;
3. That all socialist parties abandon their policy of ignoring the crimes of Russian Tsarism, and renew their support of the struggle against Tsarism, which is conducted by Russian workers without fear of any sacrifices;
4. That, in fulfilment of the resolutions of the Basle Congress, it be declared that we extend our hand to those revolutionary Social-Democrats of Germany and Austria who replied to the declarations of war by preparing propaganda in favour of revolutionary action. Votes for military appropriations must be absolutely condemned.'

It said that these demands should be met before entering into any discussions as to the re-establishment of the International. – Lenin's *Collected Works*, vol. xviii, p. 142.

class elements in opposition to the dominant military Imperialism.'

After the Russian Revolution in March, 1917, the Petrograd Workmen's and Soldiers' Council issued an invitation for a working-class International Conference at Stockholm. Mr. Henderson, the principal spokesman of Labour, opposed, though Mr. Lloyd George was in favour of the Conference. The Government sent Mr. Henderson to Petrograd to ensure, if possible, the continuation of Russia in the war. There, he changed his mind concerning the advisability of the Stockholm Conference.

The Labour Party Conference in August, 1917, approved of participation in the Stockholm Conference. Mr. Lloyd George and his Government changed their views of the conference, fearing the revolutionary effect upon the workers of the Allied Powers.

Mr. Henderson resigned from the Cabinet. Mr. Barnes took his place. 'The Executive Committee of the Labour Party, in alliance with the Parliamentary Committee of the Trade Union Congress, then applied itself to getting agreement among the Labour and Socialist Movements of the Allied Nations as to the lines – *assuming an Allied victory* – on which the terms of peace should be drawn, in order to avert as much as possible of the widespread misery, which, it could be foreseen, must necessarily fall upon the wage-earning class. In this effort, in which Mr. Henderson displayed great tact and patience, he had the *implicit sanction of the British Government* . . .'[1]

On December 28th, 1917, a Joint Conference of the Trades Union Congress and Labour Party agreed upon a statement of *war aims* approved by Mr. Lloyd George

[1] *History of Trade Unionism*, p. 695.

and 'made the basis of President Wilson's celebrated "Fourteen Points".'

The completeness of the accord between the Labour Party and trade union leaders and the British Imperialist Government cannot therefore be questioned. Their subordination of the Socialist and Trade Union Movement to 'winning the war' stands in contrast with their pledge to the Basle International Socialist Congress. Their policy consisted in the suppression of revolts, strikes, and all forms of anti-militarism within the British Empire and Allied countries, and the encouragement of revolt and all forms of anti-militarism in the 'enemy' countries.

When the Russian Revolution took place in March, 1917, they estimated it wrongly, as did the British Government. Hence both of them welcomed it in the hope of a more vigorous prosecution of the war on the Russian front. After the Bolshevik Revolution in November, 1917, the Labour Party Conference held in January, 1918, welcomed Litvinoff because the leaders had not had time to marshal their forces and dare not affront the working-class support of the Russian Revolution. By July, 1918, it was Mr. Henderson and his colleagues who organized, amidst great uproar, the refusal of the Labour Party Conference to hear Litvinoff. But Kerensky, the spokesman of the capitalist revolution against the Russian working class, who was anxious to plunge the Russian workers once more into the war, was secured a hearing.

It may be argued that the leaders had the support of the majority of the organized workers throughout the war. That is true. Social mass movements are not mere debating clubs. Once the Labour Movement had broken itself against the fact of war without producing a new leadership expressing its opposition to the war, the old leadership was aided in the maintenance of its grip by the governmental allies they had made, the fears of invasion, the loyalties 'to the lads at the front', and a thousand and one factors associated with the process of war. Added to all these factors was the general political immaturity of the independent movement of the working class.

The new movement of opposition to the war could only grow out of the sufferings and disillusionment which the prosecution of the war brought in its trail, out of the resentment against the violation of agreements and the destruction of trade practices established after years of struggle. The development of the coherent organized opposition was retarded by the policy of the revolutionaries. Movements grew spontaneously but were held back by sectarian ideas of the revolutionary leaders.

By 1918, however, the opposition to the war and support for the Russian Revolution was definitely focused in the Labour Party itself by the British Socialist Party and a section of the I.L.P. At the Labour Party Conference in January of that year they were responsible for the mobilization of 700,000 votes in favour of the Labour Party withdrawing from the Government.

Two other important factors entered into the calculations of the Labour leaders. These were – the great increase of trade union affiliations which accompanied the growing militancy of the masses and the political discontent in the ranks of the middle class. The women's suffrage movement which had become exceedingly militant just prior to the war showed that the dissatisfaction with the old parties was not confined to the working class. But there was no avenue for the middle class to move into the Labour Party other than through the I.L.P. and the Fabian Society.

The Labour Party leaders saw in this situation an opportunity to stem the tide of revolutionary feeling in the ranks of the workers. Steeped as they were in Liberalism they welcomed the chance of reinforcements and opened the doors of the Labour Party to the middle classes by means of individual membership. Mr. Webb says of the change made in the constitution of the Labour Party in 1918, that it 'transformed the Labour Party from a group representing the *class interests of the manual workers* into a fully constituted political Party of national scope, ready to take over the Government of the country and to conduct both home and foreign affairs on definite principles.'

Max Beer in his *History of British Socialism* says of this development:

> 'For the reconstruction on socialist lines, the Labour Party stood in need of social economic knowledge. And there were men and women with that knowledge, middle class intellectuals, who had cut themselves adrift from their class and sought admission to the Labour Party, but whose strait gate did not allow them to enter freely, since the old constitution of the Labour Party has been made mainly for manual workers. Things shaped themselves as Marx foresaw when he declared that "in times when the class struggle is nearing the decisive hour . . . a portion of the middle class ideologists, those who have raised themselves to the level of comprehending theoretically the historical movement as a whole, joins with the revolutionary class, the class that holds the future in its hands." To

allow them to join the Labour Party and supply the necessary knowledge to the proper instrument of reconstruction, a reorganization or a new constitution of the Labour Party was necessary. . . .'

At no stage however did the Labour Party represent 'merely the class interests of the manual workers' although its social composition was overwhelmingly that of manual workers. It was actually a mobilization of the working class under the banner of working-class independence. But the banner was carried by Liberal-Labour leaders. The feet of the movement were shod with proletarian boots but its head was still Gladstonian wearing a little red cap which it liked none too well.

The change therefore was not quite the change indicated by Mr. Beer. The influx of the middle class intellectuals was not for the purpose of helping the 'revolutionary class to power', but to prevent it getting to power, to bring it more securely under the control of liberalism.

As a movement of social forces it may be described as the growth of an alliance of the working class and the middle class, but the leaders repudiated the revolutionary implications of such an alliance. They put forward the alternative of the Labour Party as a 'National Labour Party' that could step into the shoes of the decaying Liberal Party. This meant the subordination of the working class to the middle class.

At the same time they could not entirely escape from the socialist aspirations of the masses and they therefore proclaimed the Labour Party to be a Socialist Party. Their socialism, however, was of such a confusing and compromising character that no one can describe the aims set out in the new constitution or the Programme launched at the Conference as fundamental socialist documents. Both were documents of political expediency aiming at the gathering in of forces to the Labour Party and antagonizing nobody.

The aim was set forth as follows:

> 'To secure for the producers by hand or by brain the full fruits of their industry, and the most equitable distribution thereof that may be possible, upon the basis of common ownership of the means of production and the best obtainable system of popular administration and control of each industry and service.
>
> Generally to promote the political, social, and economic emancipation of the people, and more particularly of those who depend directly upon their own exertions by hand or by brain for the means of life.'

This omnibus declaration, a typical compromise formulation open to a variety of interpretations, illustrates the outlook of the leaders at this time. What is a producer by hand? What is a producer by brain? Do those who use their hands not use their brains? Do those who use their brains not use their hands? What are the 'full fruits of their industry?' What is the 'most equitable distribution thereof?' What does 'the common ownership of the means of production' mean? Does it mean 'State capitalism' or 'Public Corporations' or 'Social Ownership?'

The ambiguity of expression in every sentence was, of course, a calculated ambiguity to give scope for socialist perorations which would appeal to the masses, and to facilitate 'practical reformist politics' from wherever they may come.

The 'Constructive Programme' which was the first effort of the Labour leaders to translate these aims into everyday politics was outlined by Mr. Sidney Webb in *Labour and the New Social Order*. It was a typical Fabian document. It proposed to begin by introducing a series of reforms such as the 'enforcement of the National Minimum wage', 'the universal application of a prescribed minimum of health, leisure, education and subsistence' by the extention of such legislation as the Factory Acts, Public Health Acts, Housing Acts, Education Acts, Trade Boards Acts. Then 'tentatively and gradually to nationalize those industries which have reached the most advanced stage of monopoly and concentration'. It also proposed the 'democratic control of industry', the utilization of the surplus wealth for the National Good, a Capital Levy to pay off a substantial part of the National Debt. Its imperial policy consisted of Home Rule and Democratic Self-Government within the Empire. Its foreign policy supported a Universal League of Nations, International Arbitration and Conciliation.

Immediate reforms stood in the foreground. Socialism was regarded as something afar off. The middle classes had no need to fear drastic measures. The workers were assured that Mr. Lloyd George was not the only one who could promise 'homes fit for heroes to live in'.

With one accord the leaders, Messrs. Webb, MacDonald, Snowden, Clynes, Thomas, Henderson and others, proclaimed that 'the Labour Party is not a class party but a National Party'. How different is the note from that struck in the days of the agitation for the formation of the Labour Party when even the Fabian Society in 1892 called loudly in its published election manifesto to the working men to 'quicken the pace towards a genuine "working-class party".'[1]

[1] Fabian Tract No. 40 referred to by M. Beer in his *History of British Socialism*, p. 301.

How different too, from the speeches and resolutions of the Leeds convention in 1917!

Nevertheless the new constitution of the Labour Party in many respects represents a decided advance of the working-class movement. The formation of Local Labour Parties based upon individual membership could not be confined to the middle classes, and large numbers of workers and their wives came into its ranks. They were not coming in because they had read the new programme of the Labour Party. They came into it because they wanted a party of their own to fight their daily battles against the capitalists. It is this fact which stands out most significantly, marking the advance of the working class in the development of its own independent political party. By the end of 1918 the Labour Party with its trade union affiliations had three million members. The influx of middle-class members did not change the working-class foundations of the party.

The significance of this development was not lost on the capitalist class. Nor was the temper of the movement misunderstood. The spread of the revolutionary wave across Europe thrilled the working class of Britain too. By the autumn of 1918 there was no hesitation in the Labour Party Conference on the question of the Labour Party's withdrawal from the Coalition Government. It decided by an overwhelming vote to withdraw from the Government and to resume its independent course.

It was this fact and the correctness of his appraisement of the class relations existing in the international situation which led Mr. Lloyd George to plunge into the Khaki election of 1918. He and his Government determined on a counter class mobilization. They knew that once the army was demobilized and the anticipated post war economic crisis arrived the discontented masses would flow to the Labour Party in a mighty stream. Class would confront class on a scale greater than England had ever known. Delay, they knew, would be fatal. The Government must be in an unchallengeable position of authority, moral as well as physical, to meet the crisis.

In a memorandum to the Versailles Conference in 1919 Mr. Lloyd George wrote:

> 'Europe is filled with revolutionary ideas. A feeling not of depression, but of passion and revolt reigns in the breasts of the working class against the conditions of life that prevailed before the war. The whole of the existing system, political social and economic, is regarded with distrust by the whole population of Europe. In some countries, like Germany and Russia, this unrest is leading to open revolt and in others, like France, England and Italy it is expressed in strikes and in a certain aversion to work. All signs go to show that the striving is as much for social and political changes as for increases in wages.'

There can be little doubt, in view of the course taken by him and his Government, that this represented his view of the situation at the end of 1918 also. Hence the decision for the Khaki election which split the Liberal Party and returned 57 Labour representatives supported by a vote of 2,244,948. It also secured an overwhelming coalition majority.

Thus once more Mr. Lloyd George had secured an advantageous manœuvring position against the rising working class. He had succeeded on the previous occasion, by his Limehouse campaign and legislation, in retarding the political development of the Labour Party and postponing the demise of the Liberal Party. But the class mobilization continued. In 1918 he broke the Liberal Party in a desperate effort to confront the advancing working class with a united capitalist combination. One more desperate effort he had yet to make before the Liberal Party lay in ruins and Mr. Lloyd George himself was dropped from the leadership of British capitalism.

This was in March, 1920, when he appealed to the Asquith Liberals to join him in Coalition with the Tories. He said:

> 'The new danger was known as Socialism in Germany, as Bolshevism in Russia. In Britain it is the Labour Party which strives for the collective ownership of the means of production. For the Liberals this is unacceptable in principle, as the Liberals are for private property . . . Civilization is in jeopardy . . . The Liberals and Tories must unite . . . If you go to the agricultural areas, I agree that you have the old party divisions as strong as ever. It does not walk in their lanes. But when they see it they will be as strong as some of these industrial constituencies now are.
>
> 'Four-fifths of this country is industrial and commercial; hardly one-fifth is agricultural. It is one of the things I have constantly in mind when I think of the dangers of the future here. In France the population is agricultural and you have a solid body of opinion which does not move rapidly, and which is not easily excited by revolutionary movements. That is not the case here. This country is more top-heavy than any country

in the world, and if it begins to rock, the crash here, for that reason, will be greater than in any other land."[1]

This clear presentation of class relations and the recognition of the full significance of the growth of the Labour Movement governed the Khaki election and all subsequent political manœuvres of the capitalist class. It was the first decisive step of the ruling class in its preparations to meet the oncoming storm.

But the Labour Movement was not in so fortunate a position. Its leaders had not so clear a vision of the relation of class forces nor did their political conceptions inspire them to lead the working class on the principles of the class struggle. They wanted 'peace', the placid flow of events which would give time for 'mutual friendly understandings' between the classes. 'There ought to be no class war,' they said, 'but a quiet talk around the conference table'. Hence every struggle was 'regrettable' and they regarded their task as that of holding the workers in leash, separating the actions of the unions instead of uniting them for common action, propaganda speeches instead of a united class answer to the coalition of capitalist parties.

They did not believe that the Bolshevik Revolution signified more than a violent revolt against peculiarly Russian conditions. They were of the opinion that it would quieten down into a second edition of the French Revolution. It did not mean to them that the Russian Revolution was the beginning of the World Revolution. They were convinced of the possibility and probability of the restoration of capitalism everywhere. Their policy

[1] *Manchester Guardian,* March 19th, 1920.

was therefore based upon trade recovery and a gradual amelioration of capitalism and its reform into socialism. Their estimate of the situation was a typical Liberal estimate. Their policy was a typical Liberal policy. They functioned as the Left Wing of the capitalist class in charge of the working class – a dangerous and fateful role when revolution is on the way, but one which acted as a breaker on the revolutionary class advance of the workers.

CHAPTER X

RETREAT OF CAPITALISM

HARDLY had the noise of the Khaki election died away when the working class began its great offensive against capitalism with the 'Forty Hour' Strike in the Clyde district of Scotland in January, 1919. The Clyde Workers' Committee had once more got into its stride and its influence extended into industries other than engineering. The Scottish miners especially had come under its influence, through the establishment of Miners' Reform Committees on the lines of the reform committees among the South Wales miners. These spread through the Lanarkshire, Lothian and Fife Coalfields. They were demanding a 'five day week', a 'six hour' working day; the abolition of piece work and the 'direct control of the industry by the workers'.

The agitation also reached the dockyards of the Clyde. The trade unions became increasingly sympathetic. A joint committee of the local union committees and the Clyde workers' committee was established to centralize the campaign for a 'forty hour working week', in order to absorb the unemployed. The Scottish Trades Union Congress, the Glasgow Trades Council and the Engineering and Shipbuilding Federation supported the demand.

The C.W.C. has been criticized for uniting with the trade union officials. This, however, was not a mistake. Had it attempted to lead the strike independently it would have crippled the strike at its inception. Its greatest mistake lay in the fact that it had done nothing to prepare the movement beyond the Clyde. Although it was represented on the National Committee of the Shop Stewards, it had not even acquainted this committee of its plans. The workers' committees and the shop stewards were left in the lurch. Despite that, the National Committee at once gave the call for support to the Clyde and all over the country strenuous efforts were made to rally support for the strike.

Sixty thousands workers in Glasgow responded to the strike call[1] issued by the Joint Committee. On January

[1] The strike call. CALL TO ARMS! To the Workers

The Joint Committee, representing the official and unofficial sections of the industrial movement, having carefully considered the reports of the shop stewards and representatives of the various industries hereby resolve to

DEMAND A FORTY HOUR MAXIMUM WORKING WEEK

for all workers as an experiment with the object of absorbing the unemployed. If a forty hour week fails to give the desired result, a more drastic reduction of hours will be demanded.

A General Strike has been declared to take place on Monday the 27th of January and all workers are expected to respond.

By order of the Joint Committee representing all industries.

Sub-Committee:

Hugh Lyon	J. Campbell	G. Marshall
J. Thom	J. Burns	G. Campbell
J. Auld	D. Rennie	J. Maloney
A. Hopkins	W. Kerr	D. Kerr (Councillor)

E. Shinwell (Councillor), Chairman.

S. Nimlin, G. S. Morton, W. Shaw — Joint Secretaries.

Demand a FORTY HOUR week Now!

Thousands are being demobilized from the army and navy every day. Over 100,000 workers have been dismissed from civil employment.

They are looking for jobs.
There are no jobs for them.
There is only one remedy.
Reduce the number of hours.
The time for action is now.
Delay means failure.
No more than 40 hours to be worked per week.
No overtime to be worked.
No work on Monday, 27th January.
No resumption of work until demands are conceded.

By order of Joint Committee.

28th a special Conference was held in Glasgow at which 700 delegates attended from the Clyde District and many towns throughout Scotland. It passed the following resolution:

> 'This Conference pledges its support to the Joint Committee and urges it to prosecute the strike with the utmost vigour until the Government is forced to open up negotiations with the Joint Committee, and when they have done so, to submit their proposals to the rank and file with a view to a satisfactory settlement on the basis of a forty-hour week for all, with no reductions in wages to time or piece workers.'

On the following day a great demonstration was held in St. George's Square, Glasgow, where the Municipal buildings are situated. The Lord Provost of Glasgow received a deputation from the strikers and offered to appeal to the Government in the matter and promised to meet them again on February 1st.

The next day the Scottish Trades Union Congress met and called for a general strike throughout Scotland. This gave a great impetus to the whole movement. Mass pickets marched from one firm to another throughout Glasgow. The strike committee issued a daily bulletin in which it gave the reports from the districts day by day.

The wide sweep of the strike can be gathered from these daily cryptic messages. 'A mass picket was successful in inducing the workers of Singer's factory to stop work on Wednesday. This involves 11,000–12,000 men and women.' 'The Firth Strike Committee report that about 14,000 men are on strike.' 'Paisley all out on strike except mills which will surely follow.' 'The Lanarkshire miners mean business and all the pits in the county were idle yesterday by arrangement with the Executive and the Reform Committees. The Executive was at first opposed to the Reform Committees. The Executive was at first opposed to the strike until the rank and file marched into Hamilton, occupied the union offices and demanded that the executive capitulate.' 'The Dumbarton Strike Committee reports that a local cinema proprietor refused the use of the place for a strikers' meeting, with the result that a boycott of his two cinemas was enforced on Tuesday, and on Wednesday he offered the picture house for a strikers' meeting.' 'Over sixty thousand men are on strike in Belfast and 100,000 are idle. The city is practically in the hands of the strikers.'

On February 1st a mighty demonstration led by Gallacher, Kirkwood and Shinwell assembled to hear the report of the Lord Provost as promised. A deputation headed by Gallacher and Kirkwood entered the City Chambers. Instead of reporting to the deputation the Lord Provost came out of the building, read the Riot Act and launched the prepared police force upon the crowd. As Gallacher and Kirkwood dashed out the police floored them with smashing truncheon blows.

By the evening of the same day the centre of the City of Glasgow was an armed camp. Thousands of soldiers were drafted into the city with machine guns and tanks. The Square was barricaded and the railway station guarded as if the city were besieged. Gallacher, Kirkwood and Shinwell were arrested on the charge of 'inciting to riot'.

The joint committee issued a manifesto entitled 'An appeal to British Labour'. In place of the arrested leaders new men were brought on to the committee. Protests against police brutality were numerous and widespread.

The Barrow engineers struck work on February 5th. London engineers decided to strike on February 6th.

But the tempo of the movement slackened. The other districts where the shop stewards' and workers' committees were conducting a vigorous campaign for support were finding the ground too unprepared. When the executive of the Amalgamated Society of Engineers condemned the strike and suspended the Glasgow District Committee, the engineering shop stewards were faced with a strong counter campaign from the officials who pleaded that the 'precipitate action on the Clyde was jeopardizing the national movement for reduction of hours'.

On February 11th the strike was called off. Gallacher and Kirkwood were sentenced to six months imprisonment, and Shinwell to three months.

The strike did not succeed in its immediate aim. But it certainly set the pace for the working class throughout the country. It showed that a tremendous amount of pent up energy in the working class was ready to be let loose. The capacity of the trade union leaders to hold back the workers from simultaneous mass action was about to be taxed to the utmost.

In this they were assisted by the Government and the employers who manœuvred cleverly. Retreating before the pressure of the masses, who in all industries were pushing forward with demands for reductions of hours of labour and advances in wages, they pursued the policy of dividing to conquer. They conceded as from February 1st, 1919, the 48-hour week for railwaymen, thereby fulfilling a pledge made during the war. The Engineering and Shipbuilding workers secured a reduction of hours from fifty-four per week to forty-seven per week. The

Cotton operatives secured a reduction of hours from fifty-five and a half hours per week to forty-eight. The eight-hour shift was granted to the Iron and Steel workers.

These concessions left the Government free to deal with the miners who were demanding increased wages, shorter hours, the nationalization of the mines and the democratic control of the industry. The Government and mine owners were in a tight corner. The stocks of coal were exceedingly low. The demobilization of the army was pouring thousands of soldiers back into the mining villages and industrial towns. Discontent amongst them was widespread. The Triple Alliance was giving moral support to the claims of the miners.

The Government made two important moves. In return for the postponement of strike notices of the miners on February 27th it agreed to the setting up of a Royal Commission on the Coal Industry on which the miners were allowed to nominate or approve the choice of half the members, excluding the chairman — Mr. Justice Sankey.

The publicity side of this commission's work was most effectively used by the Labour representatives to conduct the most exhaustive and scathing exposure of capitalist industry. The Commission had to admit that the existing system of ownership stood condemned and that some new system of public ownership ought to take its place.

But this moral condemnation of the system did not worry the Government. They were more concerned about the mass attack of the workers upon the system. The talking time of the Commission they regarded as profitable time, let the Commission say what they might. So long as the miners were kept at work, each day was a gain to the Government and the mine owners. When they conceded two shillings per shift increase of wages, and reduced the hours for underground workers from eight to seven per shift, a month later, they not only prevented a strike, but transformed the demands of the miners for nationalization of the mines and the democratic control of the industry into mere propaganda. Having done that, not all the subsequent campaigning of the Labour Party and the trade unions could re-transform these demands into issues which would secure mass action.

The Government was not so successful in its second manœuvre. It repeated the war time trick of convening a National Industrial Conference of employers and trade unions. But the Miners, Railwaymen and Transport Workers and the Amalgamated Society of Engineers refused to have anything to do with it. This practically reduced the conference to the position of an unrepresentative body. A number of the less important unions remained in it. The Government made promises to them which were never fulfilled. The main purpose of this conference was to kill time by keeping the trade union leaders talking as in the case of the Coal Commission.

They not only kept talking but also divided, each union making its own bargain on the strength of the general militancy of the working class as a whole. The centralized leadership of the capitalist class stood in marked contrast to that of the Labour Movement. Although the latter was on the offensive it was led by those who feared the implications of common action on the part of the working class.

Hardly had the mining crisis subsided when in June the cotton workers struck on a question of wages. In July 150,000 Yorkshire miners went on strike for higher wages. The strike lasted nearly a month. Troops and naval ratings were sent to the coalfield but to little avail.

In the same month the Police Strike against the Government Bill prohibiting trade unionism in the police force took place. This strike was provoked by the Government for the purpose of ridding the police force of radical elements. The strike was only partial and centred in London and Liverpool. The Government was therefore easily able to 'cleanse' the force of the strikers and proceed with measures for its re-organization as a more 'loyal' body.

This was the beginning of the process which has culminated in the Trenchard measures of 1933 for the transformation of the police into a 'class' proof militarized arm of the State.

In September the great railway strike for the raising of the wages of all grades took place. In 1913 the average wage of a railway worker was 28 shillings for a working week of about 60 hours. Owing to the great advance in the cost of living wages were increased during the war by a bonus which at the end of 1918 amounted to thirty-three shillings a week on the original basic wages. The union now demanded the highest standard rate for each grade then existing plus thirty-three shillings war wage, with a minimum of £3 a week.

The Government were determined to resist the demands. Mr. Lloyd George admitted that the Government had been preparing for the strike since the previous February. The strike lasted nine days. It was denounced by Mr. Lloyd George and his colleagues as an 'anarchist conspiracy'. The strike certainly aroused the world of labour. Revolutionary language became quite commonplace. But the leaders of the N.U.R., especially Mr. Thomas, kept a firm control of the union, which did not even appeal to the Triple Alliance of which it was a member, for any assistance. A settlement was reached on October 5th.

Although the counter measures of the Government for an alternative transport service proved very feeble this was the occasion on which the Government started to organize a permanent machine for coping with transport and general strikes. It was the beginning of the Organization for the Maintenance of Supplies which was to figure so prominently in 1926 during the General Strike.

The railway strike was followed by the strike of Ironmoulders and Coremakers—65,000 workers were on strike for 105 days. They demanded fifteen shillings per week increase and seven shillings and sixpence increase for apprentices. They secured after the long dispute only five shillings per week increase.

Numerous smaller strikes took place afterwards. In October, 1920, the miners called a national stoppage of the mines to force a further increase in wages. The Triple Alliance threatened action in support of the miners and on October 21st the National Union of Railwaymen issued provisional notices for a strike of its members to take effect on October 24th. With the agreement of the miners this strike threat was not carried into effect. The strike, begun on October 18th, was called off on November 3rd with a concession of two shillings per shift and a temporary agreement until March, 1921.

In this strike the Government added a new weapon to its armoury for dealing with strikes. This was the Emergency Powers Act. This Act, which received the Royal Assent on October 29th, 1920, enabled the Government, on the threat of any action calculated 'to deprive the community, or any substantial portion of the community, of the means of life', to declare a 'state of emergency'. On the issue of such a proclamation, the Government was empowered, by Order in Council, to take any steps it deemed necessary. It was passed as a permanent measure. The Government evidently had an eye on the future as well as the immediate situation.

During 1919 and 1920 the strike wave reached tremendous proportions. In 1919 there were not less than 34,903,000 days of strike action. In 1920 there were 27,111,000. The trade unions increased their membership to 8,328,000. The Labour Party affiliations rose to 4,359,807. Never had the working class of this country been so mightily organized nor had mass action been on a greater scale.

More important still was the character of the political ferment which developed during these years and penetrated every phase of working-class activity. Revolutionary ideas were exceedingly popular. Demands for the nationalization of this and that industry were accompanied by the demand for 'Workers control of industry'. Despite the known sympathies of the leaders of the Labour Party for Kerensky and his supporters the working class was definitely on the side of the Russian Revolution.

So great was the influence of the Revolution that many workers and 'left' leaders were thinking of the possibilities of an immediate revolution in Britain. All sections of the organized labour movement were discussing the 'problems of transition'. Even Mr. and Mrs. Sydney Webb felt impelled to write in their new edition of the *History of Trade Unionism* that 'the new legitimate and desirable movement, especially characteristic of the present century, for the increased direct participation in management of the associations of producers – whether of professional societies of trade unions, or doctors or teachers, or miners and railwaymen – has not been in this or any other country, anything like exhausted. In our view, in fact, it is along these lines that the next developments are to be expected'.

The shop stewards were no longer having to debate with railwaymen and miners concerning the application of their principles of 'organization on the job'. Both miners and railwaymen were busy adapting schemes of the shop stewards to their respective industries.

The National Guildsmen, who were a radical offshoot of the Fabians, published a great deal about 'Self-government in industry', and were responsible for some very interesting experiments in guild organization amongst the building workers. These were organizations of workers who through their trade unions organized themselves for making direct contracts for building schemes. During 1920 and 1921 they contracted for £2,000,000 of work. But they proved incapable of overcoming the difficulties of raising the necessary capital especially when the slump came.

The main scheme of the National Guildsmen consisted of the organization of the trade unions into industrial unions for the purpose of controlling industry through an industral parliament and workshop committees. The industrial parliament however had to be subordinated to a consumers' parliament representative of the 'nation'. Their goal had to be reached by means of 'encroaching control', that is, by steady organization 'on the job'.

The shop stewards' movement was caught in this stream too. W. Gallacher, chairman of the Clyde Workers' Committee, and J. Paton, jointly issued a memorandum entitled 'Towards Industrial Democracy'. This document said:

> 'There is only one thing to be done and we can begin to do it *now*. It is to smash the wage system and wrest the control of industry from the capitalists. Nothing else is of use at all . . . the movement for the overthrow of capitalism by an abolition of the wages system must begin, not at Westminster, not in the Trade Union Executive, nor yet in the trade union branches, but in the workshops. And it should take the form of the assumption by the workers of an ever-increasing share in control.'

After outlining how they believed the workshop and industrial committees would function after the workers had secured control they defined the next steps. They said:

> 'Only the apathy or disloyalty of the workers themselves can prevent the Works' Committee having in a very short time the experience and authority to enable them to undertake in one large contract, or in two or three contracts at most, the entire production throughout the establishment . . . The contract price or wages – for it is still wages – will be remitted by the firm to the Works' Committee in a lump sum, and be distributed by the workers' representatives or their officials to the workers, by whatever system or scale of remuneration they choose to adopt.'

This of course is but an attempt at modernizing what Connolly had written in *Socialism made Easy*.

A little later on there was an attempt to adapt the shop stewards' movement to the soviets as seen in the Russian Revolution. It was thought possible by building what were called 'social committees' and attaching them to the workshop committees that soviets would be evolved. This theory was advanced in a pamphlet by J. R. Campbell and W. Gallacher entitled 'Direct Action'. After outlining the structure of the shop stewards' and workers' committee organization as propagated by the shop stewards, this pamphlet said:

> 'As the industrial struggle grows more intense the workers realize the need for supplementing their industrial organizations by creating social organizations. In other words, it will be found necessary to organize the workers in the place where they live as well as in the place where they work.
>
> . . . The ultimate functions of this social organization, composed of committees organized where the worker resides, would be to supersede the existing social organization of capitalism, and to organize the social side of the workers' life, but they also have immediate work to perform in furthering the workers' struggle for power. . . .
>
> In the first place they can act as an agency for supplying food to strikers . . . collect money subscriptions for workers on strike, establishing a depot for receiving gifts of food from other workers; arranging for strikers' children to be boarded out with families not immediately affected by the strike; bring pressure upon co-operatives to assist strikers. . . .
>
> Another function of the social committees would be to take an inventory of the industries of the neighbourhood in which it is operating. . . .'

The Clyde Workers' Committee published this pamphlet and proceeded with the attempt to form 'social committees'. The English section of the shop stewards' movement rejected these ideas. The leaders of the English Movement held the view that soviets can be created by the masses only when the historical situation is such that the masses are involved in their creation in the midst of a revolutionary situation. Any attempt by a revolutionary minority to form them under other conditions would result only in the formation of propaganda groups favourable to soviets, but not the actual organization of soviets.

This actually happened and Gallacher himself later speaks of the social committees as units of the Communist Party in Scotland. In an article quoted by Lenin in *Left Wing Communism*, Gallacher said 'We represent the revolutionary movement in Scotland striving to build up a revolutionary organization within the different branches of industry and a Communist Party, based on *social committees* throughout the country.'

Yet amidst all the confusion in these theories of the 'right' and 'left' wings, of the Labour Movement there is one common factor. All recognized that the working class was in the ascendancy heading towards a new system of society in which the workers were to take the leading part. Messrs. Webb, MacDonald, Thomas, Clynes and Snowden certainly did not want such a workers' revolution. The revolutionaries of the left wanted the revolution but had the most confused notions as to its development and how to work for it. The Right wing were repeatedly driven by the workers into actions and situations they did not want. The Left welcomed every action but were either swallowed up in the mass movement or isolated by their sectarian and idealistic theories. Both had much to learn from the Russian Revolution and none could escape the effects of it upon the workers.

Although the British Government had welcomed the Kerensky Revolution it abhorred the Bolshevik Revolution. In July, 1918, it dispatched an expeditionary force to Archangel and Murmansk. As soon as this became widely known among the workers, angry protests against intervention came from all directions. The shop stewards, the B.S.P. and the S.L.P. had been active from the beginning of the revolution in propagating the Bolshevik peace terms. Large demonstrations and conferences were organized in all the big industrial centres of the country. The I.L.P. issued a manifesto against intervention. On November 4th the London Labour Party organized a demonstration in the Albert Hall which became a demonstration in favour of the Bolsheviks and the German Revolution.

Nor was the agitation kept away from the strike movements of this period. During the railway strike of 1919 branches of the railwaymen protested against intervention and called for the refusal to transport munitions, supplies and troops. On November 7th, 1919, a national 'Hands off Russia' Committee was set up representative of all sections of the Labour Movement. The Miners' Federation was exceedingly active in insisting upon action against intervention. The 'Hands off Russia' committee conducted a tremendous campaign throughout the country.

By August, 1920, the question of intervention was brought to a head. The Red armies had swept the Poles out of the Ukraine and White Russia and were pushing forward across the Polish frontiers. Lloyd George issued an ultimatum to the Soviet representatives in London that unless the Soviet armies withdrew, the British Fleet would be ordered at once to the Baltic. The indignation of the workers was roused. Inspired already by the action of the London dockers, who had refused to load the S.S. *Jolly George*, the labour movement everywhere was anxious for action.

A special Conference of the Labour Party and Trades Union Congress was called and a Council of Action set up to organize a general strike against the war. During the week-end of August 8th great demonstrations were held all over the country. Local Councils of Action sprang up from the Trades Councils and local 'Hands Off Russia Committees'. Telegrams of protest poured into the Prime Minister. On August 13th a National Conference of the Labour Party and Trades Union Congress held in London passed a resolution to resist the Intervention by a general strike. It confirmed the setting up of the Local Councils of Action for the carrying through of the strike. Telegrams were sent from the Conference to the workers of France and Italy calling upon them to join in the strike.

Before this threat the Government retreated. The British Government asked the Poles to conclude an immediate compromise with Soviet Russia and stop the war. The intervention was broken although the Government had spent £100,000,000 in support of the Counter Revolution.

Thus once more in the history of the British workers, the arch apostles of class peace had been forced into class war. They had become parties to political actions which were in flat contradiction to their theories and their policies.

The capitalist press was alarmed beyond measure. It declared that the Councils of Action were soviets. They had cause to be alarmed. They were soviets in embryo. With the capitulation of the Government they rapidly went out of existence. But their significance was not lost.

The action of the British working-class movement on the question of intervention against the Russian Revolution proved to be the crowning action of the period of its offensive. It was possibly this that made the leaders of the N.U.R. and the Miners afraid of testing the strength of the Triple Alliance in the miners' dispute of the following October. They were afraid more of its success than of its failure.

These, however, were not the only effects of the Russian Revolution on the British working-class movement during this period. New internal developments and changes in the international relations of the movement took shape and mark off the two years of offensive struggle after the war as decisive years.

CHAPTER XI

RE-BIRTH OF INTERNATIONAL WORKING-CLASS ORGANIZATION

THE years 1919–20 were decisive years in the re-birth of international working-class organization. This re-birth was not a formal affair. The war had done more than break the Second International into national fragments. All the latent differences, which before the war were smoothed over by the compromising generalship of Jaures, had divided the parties into sections and groups. The Russian Revolution accentuated the differences and forced fundamental questions into the foreground for decision and permitted of no compromise. Every country was involved in the process.

Although most of the parties of the Second International made a coalition with their respective governments for the prosecution of the war and pursued the same course as the British Labour Party, the revolutionary socialist parties and groups and anti-war socialists rapidly took steps to organize common action, which they hoped would lead to a reconstruction of the Inteinational on sounder lines. Klara Zetkin, as secretary of the Women's International Council of Socialist and Labour Organizations, convened the Zimmerwald Conference of anti-war socialists held in September, 1915.[1]

[1] Delegates to Zimmerwald.

Great Britain – The Independent Labour Party and British Socialist Party delegates were refused passports.

The countries and groups sending delegates were: Italy – Socialist Party; Russia – Bolshevik Social Democrats; Menshevik Social Democrats, Socialist Revolutionaries, and Jewish Socialist Bund; Poland – Social Democratic Party and Jewish Socialist Bund; Lithuania – Social

This conference combined in itself revolutionary socialists and pacifist socialists who had a common opposition to the war. This combination could only be temporary because the opposition to the war of necessity became something more than a humanitarian protest. Sooner or later it would mean a complete break with the existing capitalist state.

This became clear in a very short time. The Zimmerwald conference declared for the solidarity of the proletariat in face of the horrors of the war. It denounced the socialists who had lined up with their governments and called for the unity of the international working class for peace and socialism. Under the influence of Lenin the Kienthal conference held six months later went much further. It denounced 'bourgeois pacifism' as well as those who had gone over to their governments. It declared that the hope of any real peace under capitalism was an illusion. The only solution it said, 'is the conquest of political power and the ownership of capital by the peoples themselves; the real durable peace will be the fruit of triumphant socialism.'

Lenin was in favour of a new 'Third International' right from the collapse of the Second International at the outbreak of war, but this was not the view of the majority at these two conferences, although they denounced the actions of the Second International Bureau in detail. It was not until the Stockholm Conference of 1917, which failed through the refusal of passports by the Entente govern-

Democratic Party; Lettland – Social Democratic Party; Rumania – Socialist Party; and Bulgaria – 'Narrow' Socialist Party.

Unofficial Groups: France – Extreme Left Wing of the Socialist Party, Minority Section of the Federation of Labour; Germany – Minority Section of the Social Democratic Party; Sweden and Norway – Young Socialist Federation; Holland – 'De Internationale' Group; and Switzerland – Unofficial Representatives of the Swiss Socialist Party.

ments, that the decisive steps were taken for the complete rupture with the old International and the formation of the Third International.

The development of the Russian Revolution after March, 1917, forced the matter to a decision. Under the premiership of the socialist, Kerensky, the Russian Revolution was slipping out of the hands of the masses. Counter Revolution was raising its head. Kerensky forced the army into the terribly disastrous 'July offensive'. The socialist leaders of the Second International, such as Henderson of the British Labour Party and Thomas of France, were doing their utmost to drive the Russian Revolution deeper into the Imperialist War. The fate of the Revolution was at stake in the clash of fundamental principles of revolutionary and reformist socialism. It was no longer a difference of theory, which might be subordinated to some common immediate propaganda or action. It was a division involving the fate of millions upon millions of people and the subordination of socialism to imperialism and war.

Had the policy of the British Labour leaders, or that of the Independent Labour Party led by MacDonald, or the Social Democratic parties of Germany and France been accepted by the Russian workers at this stage in the history of the International working class, the Russian Revolution would have been drowned in blood. Reaction would have triumphed over Bolshevik, Menshevik and Social Revolutionary alike. The Korniloff counter-revolution would have succeeded and paved the way to Russia becoming the colonial preserve of the victorious Allied imperialists. Only the break with the reformist leaders of the Second International prevented the victory of Korniloff. It was not Kerensky who defeated Korniloff but the action of the workers under the leadership of the Bolsheviks.

The victory of Lenin among the parties and groups of Zimmerwald and the triumph of the Bolsheviks in the Revolution of November, 1917, thus made it urgently necessary to break the power of those who, at the behest of their imperialists, had led the workers into the shambles of the war and had jeopardized the Revolution. The November Revolution and the awakening of millions of the working classes of Europe and the colonial peoples which went on through many countries immediately after the war, provided the mass basis upon which the Third International was built.

The revolutionary socialists had no option in the matter. Although the coalition of the Second International leaders with their respective governments were coming to an end their political unity with the capitalist governments remained. In every country where they held control they were striving with all their might to hold back the offensive of the workers and devising ways and means to prevent any revolutionary assault upon capitalism.

The first congress of the Third International was held in Moscow in March, 1919. Its representation was limited by the difficulties imposed upon the delegates by the blockade of Soviet Russia and the war of intervention. Under the leadership of Lenin plans were made for a World Congress to be held in Moscow in the summer of 1920.

A remarkable manifesto was published by the first congress. It spoke in passionate language to the proletarians and oppressed toilers of the whole world. Signed by Lenin, Zinoviev, Trotsky, Rakovsky, and Platten, it declared:

'The new era has begun! The era of the downfall of capitalism – its internal disintegration. The epoch of the proletarian communist revolution. In some countries, victorious proletarian revolution; increasing revolutionary ferment in other lands; uprisings in the colonies; utter incapacity of the ruling classes to control the fate of peoples any longer – that is the picture of world conditions to-day.

'Humanity, whose whole culture now lies in ruins, faces the danger of complete destruction. There is only one power which can save it – the power of the proletariat. The old capitalist "order" can exist no longer. The ultimate result of the capitalist mode of production is chaos – a chaos to be overcome only by the great producing class, the proletariat. . . .

'. . . The victory of the proletariat consists in shattering the enemy's organization and organizing the proletarian power; in the destruction of the bourgeois and the upbuilding of the proletarian state machine. Not until the proletariat has achieved this victory and broken the resistance of the bourgeoisie can the former enemies of the new order be made useful, by bringing them into accord with its work. . . .'

In this declaration appears at once an estimate, fundamentally different from that of the Second International leaders, both of the era and of the task of the working class. The Second International later echoed the views of Mr. MacDonald who regarded the revolutionary movement of the masses as 'the aftermath of the war' which would pass in due course and allow social evolution to pursue its 'normal' parliamentary course. He said in his book, *Parliament and Revolution*, 'During the war many changes are born, rational and revolutionary, but they come to vigour only when the war itself has ended . . . Such is the nature of things. But this will pass, and the experience of the moment must not be regarded as normal or be made the reason for the creation of new forms of government; nor must the destructive emotions of war be carried into the peace for reconstructive purposes. . . .'

With such a conservative estimate of the situation it can hardly be a matter of surprise to find them in active collaboration with the capitalists stemming the tide of revolution.

Sixty-six parties from thirty-five countries responded to the appeal of the Third International and were represented at its second Congress held in Moscow during July, 1920. This was really the foundation Congress. In a memorable speech Lenin carried forward the work of Marx in his analysis of the era that had opened. He said:

> 'The basis of the entire situation as we find it at present, is in the economic relations of imperialism. Since the beginning of the twentieth century this new stage of capitalism, the most highly developed and last stage, has become quite clear. . . .
>
> 'The place of free competition is taken by monopolies of stupendous proportions. A mere handful of capitalists could formerly concentrate in their hands entire branches of industry; these have now passed into the hands of capitalist corporations, cartels, syndicates, trusts, which some time assume an international character. Thus with regard to finance, to rights of property, and partly to production, entire branches of industry not only in separate countries but throughout the world were captured by monopoly. . . .

'The imperialist war of 1914–18 grew inevitably from this division of the whole world, from this domination of capitalist monopoly, from this unlimited power of a mere handful of the biggest banks, say, two to five in each country. The war was waged over the question of the division of the entire world. It was waged over the question as to which of two groups of the biggest States – the British or the German – should secure opportunity and the right of robbing, crushing and exploiting the entire world. You know that the war settled this question in favour of the British group. As a result of this war all capitalist contradictions have become immeasurably more acute. . . .

'. . . If on the one hand the economic conditions of the masses have become unbearable and on the other hand increasing disintegration has set in among the insignificant minority of the all-powerful countries as illustrated by Keynes[1] then we have the ripening of both conditions making for world revolution. . . .

'. . . We have now reached the question of the revolutionary crisis forming the basis of revolutionary activity. Here we must, first of all, dwell upon two widely divergent conceptions. On the one hand bourgeois economists represent the crisis as mere "unrest", using the euphemism of the English. On the other hand, some revolutionists at times try to prove that this crisis is an absolutely hopeless one.

'This is erroneous. There are no conditions which can be hopeless. The conduct of the bourgeoisie is like that of a desperate robber who has lost his bearings. It is committing blunder on blunder, aggravating the situa-

[1] Lenin is here referring to the views of Keynes as expressed in the latter's book *The Economic Consequencces of the Peace.*

tion and hastening its own downfall. All this is true. But one cannot "prove" that there is no possibility for bourgeoisie to beguile this or that minority of the exploited, by means of some concession; that it cannot suppress this or that movement, or crush an uprising of some fraction of the exploited and oppressed. To attempt to "prove" beforehand the "absolute" hopelessness is mere pedantry, mere play of ideas and phrases. The real "proof" in this and similar questions can be derived only from experience.

'The bourgeois regime all over the world is undergoing the greatest revolutionary crisis. Now the revolutionary parties must prove by actual deeds that they possess sufficient class consciousness, sufficient power of organization, are sufficiently in touch with the masses, have enough determination and efficiency to take advantage of this crisis for a successful victorious revolution. . . .

'. . . Opportunism in the upper ranks of the Labour Movement is our greatest foe. It has been practically demonstrated that the leaders of the Labour Movement siding with the opportunists are better defenders of the bourgeoisie than the members of the bourgeoisie themselves. The latter could not have maintained itself but for the work of these leaders. . . .

'I shall dwell upon one other phase of the position. . . . We have among us not a few representatives of the revolutionary movement of the backward colonial countries. This is only a beginning, but it is important that this beginning has been made. . . .

'When the revolutionary onslaught of the exploited and the oppressed workers within each country, having overcome the resistance of their labour aristocracy will combine with the revolutionary onslaught of hundreds of millions of humanity which have hitherto been beyond the pale of history, which have been regarded as mere objects of exploitation – then imperialism will have to fall. . . .

'. . . The imperialist war has drawn the dependent nations into the arena of history. And one of our chief problems is to consider how to lay the foundation stone for the organization of the soviet movement in those non-capitalist countries. Soviets there are possible. They will be soviets not of workmen. They will be soviets of peasants, soviets of toilers. . . .

'The foundation for a soviet movement has been laid all over the East, all over Asia, among the colonial countries . . . If our international comrades will aid us now in the organization of a unified army, then no defects are going to prevent us from doing our work. This is the work of the world proletariat, the work of creating a world-wide Soviet Republic.'

On the basis of the above analysis the congress proceeded to work out in the most thorough manner the principal resolutions for the guidance of the affiliated parties. It defined the role of the Communist Party; analysed capitalist democracy and proletarian dictatorship; explained in what historical situations soviets should be formed; how communists should participate in capitalist parliaments; communist policy in relation to trade unions; the work of communists in the co-operative movement; the relation of the proletarian revolution to the liberation struggle of the colonies from imperialism.

The writer participated in this congress and was party to its decisions. Thirteen years have passed. Looking back over the experience of these years it appears clear to him that there was an over-estimation of the rapidity of the development of the world revolution and a consequent under-estimation of the strength of the leaders of the Second International in many countries. The congress and its leaders assumed that the revolutionary movement was still on the up grade and would with increasing rapidity take the workers away from the control of the Second International leaders.

At the time of the congress itself the revolutionary wave that had swept Europe had already passed its zenith and nobody recognized the fact. A more detailed study of the conditions and relation of forces and parties in each country would have proved this to be the case. It was certainly so in Britain itself. But decisions were taken on the opposite assumption. The split of the international working-class movement which the war and revolution had carried to its completion in some countries was extended to all countries whether they were ready for it or not. The general revolutionary character of the world situation and the assumption of an almost imminent world revolution was made the basis for an international split extending with equal sharpness to every country.

Had the congress examined the situation in each country and decided upon the formation of communist parties in those countries where the internal position of the working-class movement was ripe for such a decision; had it established itself as the revolutionary centre of the international working class striving to create a single international through the internal conquest of the working-class movement; it would not have thrust upon small immature groups of communists the tasks and responsibilities of independent parties and made it easy for the reactionaries to thrust them into isolation.

It was inflamed by the outrageous betrayals of the social democratic leaders in many countries, who, besides betraying the working class in the imperialist war were supporting counter revolutionary murderers. The murder of Leibknecht and Luxemburgh and many other revolutionaries was fresh in mind. It was convinced that the collapse of capitalism in many countries was imminent and that the workers were fast leaving the old leaders. Hence the decision to make the frontal attack upon the Second International by means of establishing new communist parties in each country.

So fierce became the fight between communists and social democrats that they began to hate each other more than either hated the capitalists. Thirteen years have gone by, years of gigantic struggles, and not until Hitlerism triumphed in Germany and shattered the whole organized working-class movement of that country, socialist and communist alike, is it being driven into the heads of all the parties that whatever the differences between social democrats and communists, they have a common origin in the working class and represent the working class in varying stages of evolution.

With the establishment of the Communist International there quickly followed the creation of the Red International of Labour Unions. Robert Williams, A. A. Purcell, and several leaders of the Italian trade unions, with the Russian trade union leaders, Tomsky and Lozofsky, were the initiators. They signed an agreement setting out the desirability of such a project and their willingness to participate in the task of creating this new centre of International Trade Unionism. The trade union delegates to the Second Congress of the Communist International, including the shop stewards from Britain, held a separate conference to consider the project. A provisional committee was elected for the purpose of launching a campaign against the International Federation of trade unions and organizing the First Congress of the R.I.L.U. to be held in Moscow in 1921.

Meanwhile the International Trade Union Secretariats of the unions in the various industries had been largely re-formed with a vastly increased membership. The International Federation of Trade Unions was established in July, 1919, in place of the old secretariat which had existed before the war. There were twenty million trade unionists affiliated to the new organization headed by the social democrats. With its headquarters at Amsterdam it became known as the Amsterdam International.

The re-assembling of the forces of the Second International proved to be a more difficult matter. The first steps were taken by a committee of Allied Socialists – Vandervelde, Albert Thomas, and Arthur Henderson. The intentions of the committee in convening the Berne conference of February, 1919, were really connected with securing the views of the socialist movement concerning the coming Peace Treaty. Before the conference closed there were 102 delegates present representing thirty-six countries.

But there was little agreement. The majority at once expressed their views against the Bolshevik Revolution.

They said, having learned nothing from the collapse of Liberalism, 'A re-organized society, more and more permeated with Socialism, cannot be realized, much less permanently established, unless it rests upon the triumphs of democracy and is rooted in the principles of liberty.' This was the re-affirmation of the line of the British Labour Party leaders of Socialism via Liberalism.

A section of the conference led by Adler of Austria and Longuet of France reserved their judgment on the Bolshevik Revolution. Another group, of which the Independent Labour Party was a part, stood aside and proposed the formation of another International in order to bring the Second and Third together. This became known as the 'Vienna International' and the 'Two-and-a-half International'. It really represented the left wing of the Second International steering the revolutionary workers away from the Third International into the Second. It merged with the Second International at the Hamburg Congress in 1923 when the Second International re-established itself as the Labour and Socialist International. At this Congress there were four hundred and twenty-four delegates from forty-three parties and groups. MacDonald, Thomas and Henderson represented the British Labour Party on the executive of this International.

This new situation contrasted greatly with the pre-war position of capitalism and the working class. Whereas before the war capitalism ruled throughout the world and nowhere had the workers a government of their own, the workers had, after the war, a sixth of the earth under their complete control. The workers everywhere, for the first two years after the war, were waging great revolutionary struggles and great mass strikes. Oppressed colonial peoples were shaking the power of the imperialists. A revolutionary International had been created. The old International in the custody of the imperialist socialists was resurrected.

The effect of these changes upon the British working-class movement was most profound. MacDonald and Snowden resumed their leadership of the Labour Party and strengthened the impression that the Labour Party was moving leftward after its break with the Coalition Government. The same leaders were also the leaders of the Independent Labour Party.

The latter was feeling acutely the pressure of the revolutionary events of these years. Ever since the Russian Revolution a section of this party were sympathetic to the Bolshevik policy. In 1918 Snowden headed a delegation which met with the Socialist Labour Party and the British Socialist Party to discuss the possibility of fusion. They met again in 1919 along with a delegation led by Miss Sylvia Pankhurst of the Workers' Socialist Federation.

It was obvious at these conferences that the I.L.P. delegation were there under pressure and did not agree on any of the questions of revolutionary policy. They steered clear of further unity negotiations. But the pressure grew and later the I.L.P. knocked at the door of the Communist International with an inquiry form concerning the conditions of admission. Later still a section of the I.L.P. broke away and joined the Communist Party, which had been formed by the fusion of the parties named as participating in the unity negotiations.

The inaugural Congress of the Communist Party was held in the Cannon Street Hotel, London, on July 30th, 1920. The outstanding difficulty in the way of the unity of the parties and groups who participated in this congress was that of the relations of the new party to the Labour Party. The British Socialist Party, agreeing with the basic principles of the Communist International, was in favour of affiliation. It was affiliated up to the time of the formation of the Communist Party. The rest were against. These were carrying forward the sectarian traditions of the revolutionary left that had marked its course from its beginnings in the latter part of the nineteenth century. The policy of affiliation to the Labour Party was carried by the Congress. It is doubtful whether this would have been the case had it not been for the direct intervention of Lenin[1] who wrote a letter to the Congress declaring his intention of defending this policy at the Second Congress of the Third International.

The policy of affiliation to the Labour Party was carried by one hundred votes to eighty-five against. On the return of the delegations from the Second Congress of the Third International, a further congress was organized at Leeds to bring in the groups, including the W.S.F., which had remained outside the first convention. The total membership at this time would be approximately ten thousand.

The changed situation also brought with it great changes in the position of the shop stewards' movement. The forty hour strike was the last occasion on which the shop stewards initiated and played an independent part

[1] Lenin's letter to the Communist Unity Convention:
'Having received the letter of the Joint Provisional Committee of the Communist Party of Great Britain, dated June 20th, I hasten to reply in accordance with their request, that I am in complete sympathy with their plans for the immediate organization of a Communist Party in England. I consider the policy of Comrade Sylvia Pankhurst of the W.S.F. in refusing to collaborate in the amalgamation of the B.S.P. and the S.L.P. and others into the Communist Party, to be wrong. I personally am in favour of participation in Parliament and of adhesion to the Labour Party on condition of free and independent communist activity. This policy I am going to defend at the Second Congress of the Third International on July 15th at Moscow. I consider it most desirable that a Communist Party be speedily organized on the basis of the decisions and principles of the Third International, and that the Party be brought into close touch with the I.W.W. and the Shop Stewards' Committees in order to bring about their complete union.

Lenin.

Moscow,
July 8th, 1920.

in a great strike movement. The independent activity of the trade unions and the re-transfer of workers from the engineering industry and the dismissal of active shop stewards steadily reduced the shop stewards' committees to propaganda bodies within the unions.

With the return of the delegates from Moscow the shop stewards took the initiative in the formation of a Bureau of the Red International of Labour Unions. This bureau under the chairmanship of Tom Mann drew together many prominent trade union leaders who had identified themselves with the revolutionary movement and declared themselves on the side of the Russian Revolution. Prominent among these were Robert Williams of the Transport Workers' Federation, A. Purcell of the Furnishing Trades, A. J. Cook of the Miners' Federation, Mrs. Bamber and Ellen Wilkinson of the Distributive Workers, Robert Holder of the Railway Workers, R. Coppock of the Builders' Federation, Ben Smith of the Vehicle Builders, and a number of others of the Shop Stewards' Movement. Thus the stage was set for the new developments in the British working-class movement when the great trade slump hit this country and the capitalist class were ready to begin their counter offensive against the workers.

CHAPTER XII

THE CAPITALIST COUNTER OFFENSIVE

THE autumn of the year 1920 saw the end of the working-class offensive in Britain. The capitalist class had successfully ridden the storm. Aided by the policy of the Labour and trade union leaders they had skilfully avoided a direct confrontation of classes and had dealt with the workers sectionally. Only once had they come near to a test of class strength, when, witnessing the determination of the workers on the question of the war of intervention against Soviet Russia, they retreated.

At the end of this period the workers were massed in great union battalions on a scale never before known. The Labour Party had grown to a party several millions strong. The Co-operative Movement had become one of the mightiest trading institutions in the country, successfully competing in many directions against private trade. It had revealed that its working-class instincts were strongly developed. It was propagating anti-capitalist ideas and aimed at the supersession of capitalism by the Co-operative Commonwealth. Following in the footsteps of trade unionism it had created a Co-operative Party with a similar programme and aim to that of the Labour Party.

But with all this growth of organization and power of the working-class movement it was still weighed down with leaders saturated with capitalist ideas and an outlook derived from the period of capitalist expansion. They had rallied to the defence of capitalism in war time.

Every mass attack of the workers upon the capitalists arising from the contradictory interests of the workers and capitalists was regarded by them as regrettable.

Although daily assisting the workers to build their own class organizations and parties they rejected the idea of a concerted attack of this organized power upon the forces which held the workers in subjection. They subordinated the whole movement to the theory of gradual adaptation and modification of capitalism into socialism with a minimum of friction between the robber and the robbed. They supported capitalist violence against the workers but were horrified at the idea of the workers using violence against the capitalists. They supported the Kerensky Revolution and disapproved of the Proletarian Revolution. Their support of the workers against the war of intervention was based upon liberal principles and not working-class solidarity. Their estimate of the nature of the crisis was similar to that of the Liberals. Equally with Liberals and Tories they looked forward to a trade revival as the prelude to 'normal' capitalist development in which they hoped that the Labour Party would absorb the Liberal Party in a two party system of parliamentary government. Every advance which the workers made in the direction of independent class mobilization was a direct result of the clash of interests which neither the capitalists nor the labour leaders could avoid. Indeed, the working class advanced all along the line against the capitalists despite the retarding influence and efforts of its leaders of the 'right' and the isolated sectarianism of the leaders of the 'left'.

Of course the leaders helped the workers to build their organizations. It would be stupid and foolish also to say that the great majority of them were not and are not sincere in the beliefs they hold and the policy they pursue. But it is the fate of liberalism in a world of class contradictions to contradict itself. Of the Liberals in general Marx once wrote:

> 'Although the Liberals have not carried out their principles in any land, still the attempts which have been made are sufficient to prove the uselessness of their efforts. They endeavoured to free labour, but only succeeded in subjecting it more completely under the yoke of capitalism. They aimed at setting at liberty all labour powers, and only riveted the chain of misery which held them bound; they wanted to release the bondman from the clod, and deprived him of the soil on which he stood by buying up the land; they yearned for a happy condition of society, and only created superfluity on one hand and dire want on the other; they desired for merit its own honourable reward, only to make it a slave of wealth; they wanted to abolish all monopolies, and placed in their stead the monster monopoly, Capital; they wanted to do away with all wars between nation and nation, and kindled the flames of civil war; they wanted to get rid of the State, and yet have multiplied its burdens; they wanted to make education the common property of all, and made it the privilege of the rich; they aimed at the greatest moral improvement of society, and only left it in a state of rotten immorality; they wanted to say all in a word, unbounded liberty and have produced the meanest servitude; they wanted the reverse of all they have obtained, and have thus given a proof that Liberalism in all its ramifications is nothing but a perfect Utopia."[1]

[1] *World History for Workers*, by A. Barton, p. 94.

Of Liberal Labour leaders it is only necessary to add that they endeavoured to build the Labour Movement as a movement of class peace; it has proved to be increasingly an instrument of class war. They aimed at adapting the labour movement to the requirements of capitalism, to wage its wars, restore its industry and to leave the destiny of the workers to the kind consideration of the capitalists, only to find the movement increasingly anti-capitalist, increasingly unwilling to wage capitalist war, increasingly determined to end capitalism. So long as such leadership remains at the head of the working-class movement its history must be a record of contradictions.

No wonder therefore that during the working-class offensive of 1919-20 the workers were successfully diverted from a united class attack upon the system. Nor can it be a matter of surprise that when the capitalist counter offensive began in 1921 the capitalists were able to pursue the familiar policy of dealing with one section of the workers at a time.

The counter-offensive for which the Coalition Government and the whole capitalist class had been waiting began immediately the tide of trade turned. The first big attack was launched in March, 1921, with the decision to de-control the mines and force wage reductions upon the miners. They determined on resistance in spite of the vacillations of their most prominent leader, Mr. F. Hodges.

The Triple Alliance of the miners, railwaymen and transport workers shocked the whole working-class movement by letting the miners down in the most shameful way. The Transport Federation led by Mr. R. Williams, reputed to be a revolutionary leader and one of the founders of the Red International of Labour

Unions, and the National Union of Railwaymen led by Mr. J. H. Thomas, were expected to give full support to the miners. On the fateful day, afterward known to the masses as Black Friday, the miners were left to fight a lone three months' battle which ended in defeat.

The attitude of the three principal leaders named was subsequently revealed in all its true colours. Mr. Williams complained of the faulty machinery of the Alliance and doubted whether the workers would have responded to a strike call. The judge in the court action of *Thomas* v. *MacManus and 'The Communist'* said in his summing up, 'The time came when Mr. Thomas abandoned the miners. There was no doubt about that and the jury knew the circumstances in which he did it'. The role of Mr. F. Hodges was such that he was soon driven from office. To-day Mr. Williams has ceased to play any active part in the Labour Movement. Mr. Thomas is in the Coalition 'National Government' with the Tories. Mr. Hodges has become a mineowner.

Black Friday was a calamity which affected the working-class movement profoundly. The shame and disgust which it felt played no small part in the spiritual preparation of the workers for 'Red Friday' of 1925 and the General Strike of 1926.

Before the termination of the miners' strike on July 4th a great cotton lock-out took place. The cotton workers were faced with the demand for huge wage reductions. They refused to agree to the demands of the employers. Five hundred thousand workers were locked out from June 3rd until June 27th when they resumed on the basis of 4s. 5d. reduction in the £ on current wages.

Then came the turn of the workers in the engineering industry who were involved in a fourteen weeks' lock-out which began in March, 1922. Hardly had this started when the shipbuilding workers were plunged into a defensive struggle against wage reductions. These were followed by the strike of the printing trades against a demand for 15s. a week reduction in wage rates. These defensive struggles continued in the various industries right through 1922 and 1923. During 1921 there were seven hundred and sixty-three disputes involving nearly two million workers and extending to nearly 85,000,000 days of strike action. During 1922 there were five hundred and sixty-five disputes involving five hundred and fifty thousand workers in 19,918,000 days of strikes. These figures demonstrate the tenacity of the workers in their resistance to the capitalist counter offensive.

These defeats, which in two years resulted in wage reductions to the extent of £10,000,000 a week, threw the trade union leaders especially into the deepest depression. Trade union membership rapidly declined. The Trade Union Congresses of 1921 and 1922 sank to low levels of interest. Under the pressure of these events, however, the Trades Union Congress of 1921 made an important change in its constitution. Instead of the old Parliamentary Committee it proposed the creation of a 'General Council' of the Trades Union Congress. This was announced as the formation of a 'General Staff' for the working-class movement. But true to the traditional outlook of the leaders its functions were defined, not as the means to mobilize the working class for united action against the capitalists, but to prevent the extension of disputes. The new general staff was to be a diplomatic corps to prevent struggle and not a general staff to lead the struggle of the workers.

At the 1922 Congress came the demand for 'More

Power to the General Council' in the form of giving the general council power to organize levies for the purpose of assisting the unions in disputes where necessary. This of course was an advance thrust upon the general council. It was due to the pressure of the organized Left Wing of the Trade Union Movement.

Great changes had taken place in the organization of the revolutionary forces after the establishment of the Communist Party. The shop stewards' and workers' committees at first came under the direction of the Communist Party. Then came the creation of the Red International of Labour Unions and its bureau working side by side with the shop stewards. The growth of unemployment soon liquidated the shop stewards' movement. The Bureau of the R.I.L.U. was transformed into the Minority Movement after it had completed its agitation for a strong Left Wing representation of the trade unions to the first International Congress of the R.I.L.U.

This bureau had created a wide influence within the trade unions in all the important industries and organized conferences around a programme of action for each industry. Prior to the Trade Union Congress of 1921 it issued a manifesto in which it called for the re-organization of the unions on the basis of Industrial Unionism and the reorganization of the Trades Union Congress.

Its programmes of action for the separate industries were based upon the current economic and political demands of the workers. For example, the metal workers section put forward a programme which included the demand for the 44-hour week, a national minimum wage of £4 per week, the establishment of workshop committees, one union for the industry and affiliation to the R.I.L.U. The miners, over the signatures of A. J. Cook,

S. O. Davis and W. Mainwaring, demanded the defence of the seven-hour day, a national minimum wage, the securing of the Holman Gregory report governing protection and compensation claims for the miners, the transformation of the Miners' Federation of Great Britain into an industrial union and affiliation to the R.I.L.U.

By the end of 1922 the bureau of the R.I.L.U. had 130,000 miners, 100,000 engineering workers and 70,000 outside these two industries affiliated to it. It issued a monthly paper named *All Power* with a circulation of 12,000 copies. During 1922 it launched the 'Back to the Unions' campaign which was later taken up by the Trades Union Congress. In a programme pamphlet 'Stop the Retreat' it propagated a plan for the reorganization of the Trades Union Congress in alliance with the Labour Party and the Co-operative Movement and projected the corresponding reorganization of the trades councils, local labour parties and co-operatives in three-fold local alliances.

More important from the standpoint of immediate mass action was the organization of the unemployed workers. The first Unemployed Workers' Committees were formed in London in the autumn of 1920 under the influence of communists who were ex-shop stewards. By December, 1920, there were thirty-nine committees in London representing 20,000 unemployed. It was their pressure which forced the Trades Union Congress and the Labour Party to call a special conference in the Kingsway Hall on January 27th, 1921. This conference and the subsequent Trades Union Congress which met in February, 1921, refused a hearing to the representatives of the unemployed although these assemblies were called to deal with the question of unemployment. There were at this time more than two million unemployed in the country.

In fifteen months there were three hundred committees with a contributing membership of 100,000. In 1922 the National Unemployed Workers' Committee organized the great Hunger March of 2,000 men. It began its journey on October 17th from Aberdeen, gathering its contingents together *en route* to arrive in London for the opening of Parliament on November 20th. Such a revolutionary portent had never been seen in Britain. For three weeks the whole press ignored what was taking place. But as the marchers neared London it suddenly blazed forth with hysterical announcements. The aim of the march was to send a deputation of the unemployed to meet the Prime Minister and lay their demands before him.

Scores of thousands of *workers* met the marchers in Hyde Park on November 17th, 1922. There were seventy thousand in the procession. The Prime Minister refused to meet them but the Labour leadership had to recognize that the Unemployed Workers' Committees had secured the support of the masses. The Labour Party executive and the General Council of the Trades Union Congress organized Unemployed Sunday on January 7th, 1923. They went further and established the Joint Committee of the Trades Union Congress and the National Unemployed Workers' Committees. Once more the masses had pushed the leaders in a direction they did not want to go.

This revolutionary movement in the unions and the unemployed workers finally became centred in the National Minority Movement. The name signified that its members were the organized minority within the larger movement of the working class. It was, of course, under the guidance of the Communist Party.

There was thus a great transformation of the revolutionary forces as compared with their position prior to the formation of the Communist Party. Hitherto the revolutionary parties had allowed all the various sections of the movement such as shop stewards, reform committees and the like to run, as it were, on their own, without any effective co-ordination and central leadership. They had now become centralized. They functioned principally as a Left Wing of the Labour Movement although organized independently.

It was in this period that the struggle began between the Communist Party and the Labour Party leaders. In accordance with its inaugural conference decision the Communist Party made application for affiliation to the Labour Party. This was the sequel to the decision of the Communist International to create independent Communist Parties in each country, irrespective of the ripeness of the working-class movement for the operation of such a decision. The communists were forced into an exceedingly difficult position. Before they had had the opportunity to explain the teachings of communism to the masses and to secure a wide basis of support they were forced to join issue upon questions such as 'the Dictatorship of the Proletariat', 'Capitalist democracy versus Soviets', 'the forceful overthrow of the capitalist regime'.

To suggest for a single moment that the Edinburgh Conference of the Labour Party held in 1922 was historically ready to discuss any of these questions is absurd. There had been no preparation of the movement for a discussion of these fundamentals. It was only to be expected therefore that the Labour Party leaders should at once utilize their strength to isolate the young Communist Party and set about the task of cleansing the

Labour Party of revolutionary tendencies. The Edinburgh Conference overwhelmingly rejected the Communist Party's application for affiliation and proceeded to take measures for the exclusion of its adherents from the Labour Party.

This was no easy task because, however the conference might disagree with the theoretical position of the Communist Party, it had to be recognized that at this time the revolutionaries were most closely identified with the local workers' organizations and participated most actively in all their struggles. Several years had to go by before the Labour Party, leaders succeeded in their exclusion, policy.

Had the communists at this period not formed a separate party but organized themselves as an integral part of the Labour Party, seeking to transform it from within, such an isolation of their forces would not have been possible. Their isolation is the price the revolutionary movement has had to pay for making a formal challenge on fundamental principles abstracted from the immediate struggles of the workers and without regard to the relation of forces. They thus repeated the experience of the Social Democratic Federation in 1900.

Nevertheless the revolutionaries were nearer to the feelings of the working class in this period than the leaders of the Labour Movement. They sounded the call for militant action and confidence in working-class solidarity. The stubbornness of the struggles against wage reductions during 1921 and 1922 followed by the tremendous increase in the Labour vote at the election of November, 1922, prove conclusively that the workers were not dispirited and lacking in the will to fight. But the leaders were in the depths of despair. Mr. Henderson, the secretary of the Labour Party, pleaded for 'An Industrial

Parliament: a Plea for a Pact of Peace'. Writing in the *Labour Magazine* of July, 1922, he said:

> 'It is no exaggeration to assert that the conditions of life for the workers in practically every industry are no better than they were ten years ago and that in many cases they are considerably worse.'

Did that inspire him to give the call to the working class to unite its forces and win back the losses of these ten years? Not at all. He continued:

> 'Employers should undertake not to seek to alter existing conditions by declaring a lock-out.
>
> 'Trade unions should undertake not to seek to alter existing conditions by declaring a strike.
>
> 'Changes in workshop conditions to be by mutual consent.
>
> 'Existing wage rates to be stabilized as basic with present level of cost of living registered as "normal", wages to rise automatically and periodically, in an agreed fixed ratio to increased production in each industry, so as to ensure the worker a fair share of the fruits of restored prosperity . . .'

What a remarkable rallying cry!

Then said Mr. Henderson, echoing the bankers on New Year's Day, 'I am inclined to the view that the worst phase of trade depression is behind us and that signs of recovery are gradually showing themselves'.

Within a few months of the appearance of this article the workers gave a different answer to that of the 'pact of peace', which Robert Smillie described as the 'Pact of Death'. A crisis grew in the ranks of the capitalist class as the economic crisis became more acute. The Coalition

Government resigned. In the General Election which followed in November, 1922, the Labour Party received 4,236,733 votes and 142 Labour Members and two Communist[1] Members of Parliament were elected.

This leap forward in workers' political representation when the crisis in the old capitalist parties became acute, swept the pessimism from the ranks of the Labour Movement. Immediately after the election, the Labour Party declared it was now 'on the threshold of power'. It was recognized as 'His Majesty's Opposition'. Its leaders began to pose as 'statesmen'. Mr. Snowden wrote a series of articles in the *Morning Post* (later published as a book entitled *If Labour Rules*) in which he assured everybody that 'No labour Government would ever be the Government merely of the manual labour class. The present constitution of the Parliamentary Labour Party is an answer to that fear. A considerable proportion of the party members belong to the middle classes. It contains lawyers, doctors, university professors, teachers, ministers of religion, consulting engineers, manufacturers, journalists, and even landed proprietors. A Labour Government would certainly contain many men of this type.'

He continued with his assurances, 'A Labour Government would undoubtedly disappoint its critics in one very important and vital respect. It would not be a class government. I know there will be strong pressure from certain quarters to use a Labour Government to serve the interests and meet the claims of certain sections of Labour. That, and not even the opposition of capitalist and financial interests, will be its greatest difficulty . . .'

At the same time that the most profuse assurances were

[1] The policy of the Communist Party at that time did not permit of communists opposing Labour candidates.

made that the Empire was secure, that the capitalists could sleep peacefully in their beds at night, and 'society' had no reason to be in the least perturbed at the prospect of a Labour Government, the whole of 1923 was occupied inside the Labour Party by an intensification of the campaign to exclude the communists.

MacDonald himself, who was once again the leader of the Parliamentary Labour Party, took up the fight against the communists on an international scale. Having already during 1922 played a leading part in preventing the unity of the Internationals, he now made a speciality of his defence of 'Georgia', which as a result of a Bolshevik revolution, attached itself to the Union of Soviet Republics. This he denounced as Red Imperialism. He wanted Georgia to have back its Social Democratic Government, which events proved to be an instrument of the British imperialists, who were seeking to capture the oil wells of Baku.

The attitude of the Labour Party leaders to the Russian Revolution was at this stage indistinguishable from that of General Denikin and other counter revolutionaries. These had declared themselves in favour of 'Soviets without the Bolsheviks' hoping that this would lead to 'No Soviets but a Constituent Assembly'. The Constituent Assembly was to be regarded as a stepping stone to a Parliamentary system, British model of course.

The Labour Party Conference of 1923 thought it knew the grand alternative to such uncomfortable things as Revolution. It met to formulate or rather to approve the programme of the Party on the 'threshold of Power'. Mr. Sidney Webb introduced it and made his famous speech on the 'inevitability of gradualism'. He said:

'The inevitability of gradualness cannot fail to be

appreciated. The translation of socialism into practicable objects is the task on which we have engaged for a generation, with the result that fragments of our policy have been successfully put into operation by town and county councils and the Government itself. The whole Nation has been imbibing socialism without knowing it.'

The programme included the famous demand for the 'capital levy' for the purpose of paying off a substantial amount of the National Debt. Of this proposal Mr. Snowden said, 'The proposal of a Capital Levy is just a business proposition. It is just a question whether it would be better to wipe off a considerable part of the National Debt by a lump sum payment to reduce the annual commitments for interest, or to go on paying a very high income tax for the next hundred years or more.'

'The Social Programme upon which it appealed for support,' said Mr. Snowden once more, 'will be gradually grafted on to the existing system.' It proposed to make a special feature of housing reform and stand for 'Work or full maintenance for the Unemployed'.

One after another of the leaders declared how loyal they would be to the Empire. Speaking at the British Empire Exhibition luncheon to Trade Union leaders in October, 1923, Mr. J. H. Thomas excelled himself. He said, 'We love our Empire. We are proud of the greatness of our Empire.' Mr. Clynes on the same occasion declared, 'We on the Labour side want as fervently as any class to see the British Empire well developed.' Mr. Tillett affirmed that, 'A trade basis for Empire is much better than political theorizing.'

The remainder of the Labour Party leaders took the view of Mr. Snowden. He said, 'The British Empire is a fact. We have our views about the way it has been built up. But it is a fact, and having incurred the responsibility we cannot lightly cast it off at all.'

Foreign policy consisted of support to the League of Nations, revision of the Versailles Treaty, full recognition and trade relations with Soviet Russia.

Socialism in this programme was not even skin deep. There was little to which the Liberal Party could take exception and throughout this period there were continuous efforts to win Liberals to the Labour Party as the new custodian of Liberalism.

Nevertheless the class contradictions also remained as 'Facts' which could not be ignored. The class struggle continued. The propaganda of socialism had to go on and during the 1923 Parliament a first-class debate was staged on the merits of socialism versus capitalism, in which however theoretically defective some of the contributions on socialism were, one and all on the Labour side aided in destroying the belief of masses of people in the permanency of capitalism.

More important still in thrusting the Labour Movement on to the side of the class struggle against capitalism, was the conflict of the Government with Soviet Russia and the continued attacks upon the standard of life of the workers. Trade Union leaders and Labour Party leaders had to denounce the Curzon ultimatum to Russia and threaten drastic action. This, notwithstanding the liberal character of the speeches, was fundamentally an alignment of working-class forces against capitalism. It was the determined attitude of the Labour Movement which stayed the operation of the ultimatum.

The militancy of the workers increased and more and more they thought in terms of Labour achieving political power. With this growing militancy also grew the resentment against the expulsion decisions of the Edinburgh Conference of the Labour Party directed against the communists. The Labour Party Conference of 1923 rescinded the Edinburgh resolutions restricting the right of communists to represent the trade union branches in the local labour parties and trades and labour councils. The leaders retreated to take up the question again at a more convenient moment.

By the end of 1923 the crisis in International Capitalism reached such dimensions that all the capitalist governments of Europe were faced with internal crises. In Germany the situation was so acute that a Proletarian Revolution was thought by many to be imminent, but the German working class was so divided against itself and so unprepared to strike the decisive blow that the capitalists were able to weather the storm. American, French, and British capitalism 'intervened' with financial aid and the Dawes Plan.

The crisis so reacted on the capitalist parties of France and Britain that new elections were considered necessary. These elections paved the way to what were known as governments of the Left. In Britain the General election saw another big advance of the Labour Party. On this occasion 4,348,379 voted for it and returned 191 labour members and one communist. This result made the Labour Party the largest party in Parliament.

Instead of the Tories and Liberals combining again in a Coalition Government as in the time of the Lloyd George regime, they agreed that a Labour administration should be formed, which they could tacitly control and openly dismiss the moment they thought it advisable.

Prior to the formation of the Labour Government there was a division of opinion in the Independent Labour

Party which had a majority in the Parliamentary Labour Party as to the advisability of Labour taking office without a working majority. The late Mr. Wheatley and other leaders of the I.L.P. were opposed to the proposition, but quickly capitulated, and Mr. Wheatley himself became a member of the Cabinet.

The Communist Party was in favour of the formation of such a government and called upon it to prove itself to be a 'Workers' government' by immediately bringing forward a working-class programme and challenging the opposition to defeat the Government.

But the Labour Government proceeded to disappoint most of its supporters. Its very first action was the signing of the Dawes Report, the Allied bankers' measure against the Revolution in Germany. Instead of an immediate recognition of Soviet Russia and the exchange of ambassadors, there was considerable delay. Only after an outcry from the Labour Movement did MacDonald take action and then appointed, not an ambassador, but a chargé d'affaires. Immediately negotiations opened between the two governments MacDonald put forward exactly the same demands as those previously advanced by Mr. Baldwin, viz., payment of Czarist debts to British lenders; payment of the claims of British bondholders; payment of claims of British subjects for property lost in the Revolution and no propaganda in the British Empire.

Although the Election Programme of the party declared that the Labour Party favoured 'The immediate calling by the British Government, of an International Conference (including Germany, on terms of equality) to deal with the revision of the Versailles Treaty, especially reparations and debts', Mr. MacDonald rebuked Mr. Henderson for being tactless enough to remember this, and the revision of the Treaty was transformed promptly into the maintenance of the Treaty.

When the Dockers' Strike took place in February, 1924, the Government appointed Mr. Wedgwood as chief civil commissioner under the Emergency Powers Act. The attitude of the Government so incensed the trade union leaders that after the strike collapsed Mr. Bevin said, 'I wish it had been a Tory Government in office. We would not have been frightened by their threats. We were bound to listen to the appeal of our own people.'

The most popular of its measures was the Wheatley Housing Bill. Finally it blundered into prosecuting J. R. Campbell on a charge of sedition. This caused a great outcry from the workers. It quashed the trial and by this time the Tories and the Liberals decided to force its resignation.

Despite this line of policy the advent of the Labour Government once more advanced the working-class movement along the line of the class struggle. The Labour Government, of course, had drawn a number of leading trade unionists such as Mr. Thomas, Mr. Clynes, Miss Bondfield and others away from their leading positions in the trade unions. This opened the way for the Left trade union leaders in the General Council of the Trade Union Congress. Mr. A. A. Purcell was elected chairman for the forthcoming Trades Union Congress to be held at Hull.

During the year the Trades Union Congress sent a delegation to Soviet Russia which on its return issued a remarkable report which had a profound influence on the trade unions especially. The General Council of the T.U.C. invited the Russian Trade Unions to be represented at the British Trades Union Congress.

The reception accorded to the Russian delegation led

by M. Tomsky, the chairman of the Russian Trades Union Congress, was beyond all expectation, indeed unique in the history of the British trade unions. In that reception the British workers showed how warmly they felt towards the Revolution and its achievements.

This event initiated a further development of the revolutionary forces by the creation of the Anglo-Russian Trade Union Unity Committee which pledged itself to the mutual assistance of the British and Russian workers in their struggles, and set before itself the task of achieving the unity of the two Trade Union Internationals, i.e., the International Federation of Trade Unions and the Red International of Labour Unions, to which the Russian Trade Unions were affiliated.

Before the next congress of the trade unions the Labour Government had been dismissed. The election which followed, famous for the so-called Zinoviev letter, produced the results desired by Mr. Baldwin. He was returned in strength. But the defeat of the Labour Government did not produce the reaction of pessimism in the workers' movement which parliamentarians anticipated.

On the one hand the Labour Party were successful in persuading the workers that all the mistakes were due to their being a 'Minority Government'. On the other hand the workers were facing new economic battles. The miners were in the forefront of the attack and the memory of 'Black Friday' was vividly awakened, especially when the miners under the leadership of Mr. Herbert Smith and Mr. A. J. Cook, who had superseded Mr. Hodges, appealed to the other unions for assistance so as to avoid a similar fiasco to that of 1921.

In this movement for united action the Minority Movement played a very important part. It was undoubtedly due to its influence in the Miners' Federation that A. J. Cook, who had been prominently identified with the revolutionaries for many years, was elected as General Secretary of the Federation. Six hundred delegates, representing six hundred thousand workers, attended a conference convened by the National Minority Movement in January, 1925. This conference gave the call for 'all in behind the miners'. Immediately afterwards it organized a wide agitation in the form of All-in-Conferences to prepare the common defence.

The general council of the Trades Union Congress responded to the appeal of the miners with the proposal for the formation of what was known as the 'Quadruple Alliance of Miners, Railwaymen, Transport Workers, and Engineers'. The scheme never came to anything in itself, but it led to the convening of a conference of Trade Union Executives instead of the Trades Union Congress, on the ground that the Congress itself had not the power to decide action.

Events moved swiftly forward. The employers posted notices of wage reductions to take effect on August 1st. The trades unions, pledged to support the miners, had to do something. The Special Trades Union Congress held on June 29th, called to deal with unemployment, devoted most of its time to the position of the miners.

On July 30th the Conference of Trade Union Executives met amid great excitement. The mass feeling of support for the miners swept all before it. So unique was the situation that Mr. Stephen Walsh was sent as the leader of a deputation to the Parliamentary Labour Party to make representations for the application of a policy of obstruction to all parliamentary business until the demands of the miners were met.

The conference of executives decided on the application of a complete embargo on the transport of coal in the event of the mineowners not withdrawing their notices of wage reductions. At the last moment Mr. Baldwin called a 'Nine Months Truce' on the basis of a £20,000,000 subsidy to the owners 'to enable them to maintain the exisiting agreement on miners' wages and conditions'.

This day became famous as 'Red Friday', because of the triumph of the revolutionary principle of working-class solidarity. Mr. MacDonald was outraged by the settlement. He declared:

> 'The Government have handed over the appearance at any rate of victory, to the very forces that sane, well considered, thoroughly well-examined socialism feels to be probably its greatest enemy. If the Government had fought their policy out we would have respected it. It just suddenly doubled up.'

The workers everywhere regarded 'Red Friday' as a day of victory. The revolutionaries said it was the beginning of a truce which would be utilized by the Government as a period of preparation for counter attack.

Mr. Baldwin said that 'in the event of the Trade Union threat being put into operation he would muster all the forces of the State to crush them'.

Lord Londonderry said in such circumstances, 'They would smash the unions to pieces whatever it cost in blood and treasure'.

Memorable days immediately followed 'Red Friday'. The working-class movement was keyed up to a new spirit of solidarity. Mr. George Lansbury endeavoured to crystallize the Left movement amongst the Labour forces in support of a new weekly paper, *Lansbury's Weekly*. This was supported by R. W. Postgate, J. F. Horrabin, G. D. H. Cole, and Ellen E. Wilkinson. Associated with this group were the Clyde I.L.P. leaders Maxton, Wheatley, Kirkwood and Campbell Stephen.

The Left forces, which were nearer to the Communist Party and the Minority Movement, launched the *Sunday Worker*, edited by W. Paul. It was under the guidance of the Communist Party. Prominently supporting the paper were such men as A. J. Cook and Alex Gossip.

These papers in particular conducted a powerful campaign for solidarity with the miners and preparation for the ending of the truce. So powerful was the influence of 'Red Friday' on the whole working class that no leader dare openly tell the miners that at the end of the nine months they ought to accept wage reductions. Although much discussion took place on the crisis of British capitalism, no group of leaders accepted the communist view of the crisis. Right and Left within the Labour Movement echoed the capitalist view that we were passing through temporary difficulties arising out of the war. Hence the valuation of the strike movement as merely that of making an equitable bargain with the employers and having no relation to the development of the world crisis of capitalism. Hence, also, no preparations were undertaken by the leaders of the trade unions.

The capitalist class were not so indecisive. After appointing the Samuel Commission to inquire into the coal industry once more they concentrated upon organizing their forces for civil war. The Home Secretary gave special attention to organizing the police. The 'Organization for the Maintenance of Supplies' was formed. Through this organization the middle classes were mobilized. The War Office and Admiralty were prepared.

Fascist movements were encouraged and the Conservative press maintained a persistent campaign against the unions.

Meanwhile the Second Conference of the Minority Movement was held on the eve of the Trades Union Congress which was due at Scarborough at the beginning of September. Six hundred delegates were present and it was evident that much work had been done in the trade union branches. Resolutions appeared on the agenda of the Trades Union Congress covering the questions of 'More Power to the General Council', the 'affiliation of the Trades Councils to the Trades Union Congress', the 'Affiliation of the Unemployed Workers' Committee', 'International Trade Union Unity', the 'Empire and the Liberation of the Colonial peoples'. These resolutions had been pushed forward by the Minority groups working in the trade union branches.

The Scarborough Congress was remarkable in more than one respect. On the most important political questions the Right wing, represented mainly by Mr. Thomas, Mr. Clynes, and Miss Bondfield, were defeated. The anti-imperialist resolution moved by H. Pollitt and opposed by J. H. Thomas, was carried by a majority of three million votes.

The Russian delegation was once more received with acclamation. The congress pledged itself to support the miners' demand for 'Not a penny off the pay, not a minute on the day'.

At the end of the congress the right wing were once more in the saddle. Messrs. Thomas, Clynes, and Miss Bondfield had resumed their positions at the head of the big unions, and the bloc voting of the bureaucracy brought them back into their old positions in the general council. Within a few weeks their turn came in the Labour Party

Conference held at Liverpool. It repudiated the policy resolutions of the Scarborough congress, if not in formal resolutions certainly in speech and decisions. Challenged by the Government and the capitalist press to prove that it was not a communist conference the leaders, headed by MacDonald, took the decision to bar the door to the communists completely. It invited the unions to do the same. The Lefts in the conference, fearful of being classified as communists, rendered them no support.

Immediately after the conference, Mr. Thomas wrote a special article in the capitalist press crying 'Smash them or they will smash us'. Quickly the Government obliged and arrested twelve leaders of the Communist Party on charges of seditious conspiracy under the sedition and mutiny laws of the eighteenth century. After a ten days' trial five leaders were sentenced to twelve months imprisonment and seven to six months as first offenders. The latter were offered their freedom if they would renounce the Communist Party, which they refused to do.

Instead of weakening the revolutionary movement amongst the masses this action of the Government strengthened it. It was obvious to most people that the action of the Government was related to the termination of the 'truce'. A release petition issued by the International Class War Prisoners' Association, under the chairmanship of George Lansbury, secured 300,000 signatures. Even the Labour Party had to condemn the prosecution.

But no effective preparation was made by the leaders of the unions for the coming crisis. Meetings took place between the General Council of the Trades Union Congress and the leaders of the Co-operative Movement, but nothing definite came out of them. The eve of the General Strike arrived and the union leaders were hoping against hope that something would happen to make a strike unnecessary.

When the Coal Commission Report was issued Mr. MacDonald said in *Forward* of March 19th, 1926, 'The report is a conspicuous thought . . . The stars in their courses are lighting the way for us.' These astrological opinions of the report were not echoed by the miners, who saw in the report that reductions of wages followed upon its acceptance.

Mr. Thomas openly discouraged preparations for strike action. On April the 18th, twelve days before the strike, he said, 'Instead of organizing, mobilizing and encouraging the feeling that war is inevitable let us concentrate on finding a solution.'

Despite all the actions of these gentlemen the General Strike came. The action of which revolutionaries had dreamed and which reactionaries dreaded, happened on a scale such as Britain had never seen. The leaders at the last moment had to improvise the machinery of central leadership. Three to four millions stopped work on May 1st, 1926.

Naturally such a tremendous action on the part of the workers was regarded by the Government, and rightly regarded, as a challenge to its authority, as a political challenge to the State. The General Council shrunk from such a challenge and cried that 'This is purely an industrial struggle.'

The Government made a great demonstration of armed force and brought its 'Organization for the Maintenance of Supplies' into operation. But the workers were undismayed. Everywhere the ranks were solid. They were looking forward to the development of the strike and not to capitulation. But to the consternation of the whole working-class movement the leaders surrendered at the end of nine days. The miners were left alone to face a seven months' struggle.

The Communist Party and the Minority Movement tried unavailingly to stem the return to work. But they held no decisive positions which would make that possible.

The capitulation of the trade union leaders outside the ranks of the Miners' Federation was complete. Union after union signed agreements of the most scandalous character pledging themselves never to repeat such an action. They agreed to limit themselves to their own particular industry and confine themselves to trade disputes.

But not so the miners. During the seven months struggle the influence of the revolutionaries increased within their ranks. They had no compunction, as had the general council, in accepting the financial assistance of the Russian trade unions who, true to their pledge of solidarity with the British workers in their struggles, organized voluntary collections amongst the Russian workers which in the seven months totalled not less than £1,000,000.

There can be no question of the fact that the Communist Party and the Minority Movement were responsible for the rejection by the miners of the Samuel Memorandum and the bishops' proposals, although the latter was supported by A. J. Cook, whose influence was at its highest at this time. Finally, by a great concentration of forces, they secured the turning down of the capitulation demands of the Government by 480,806 votes to 313, 200. But the leaders of the Miners' Federation were of the opinion that the strike was weakening and that the majority was not sufficient to justify the continuation of the fight.

A further success attended the campaign of the revolutionaries for the levy in support of the miners, a proposal which was backed by *Lansbury's Weekly*, as well as other left wing papers. The general council had told the Russian trade unions that a levy was not practicable. It had to report, however, that a voluntary levy realized £43,785 in eight weeks, whilst the special miners fund which they organized as an alternative realized only £9,525 in nineteen weeks. But the campaign of the revolutionaries for an embargo upon the transport of coal came to nought because it was obvious that such an embargo meant the restarting of the General Strike.

With the termination of the miners' strike an entirely new situation arrived in the Labour Movement. Reaction was in the saddle. The left forces among the trade union leaders had capitulated completely to the right. The General Council of the Trades Union Congress entered into the most friendly relations with Sir Alfred Mond and Lord Londonderry.

A veritable deluge of articles appeared in the Labour press declaring that the General Strike was a wrong weapon to use. The *Daily Herald* in a leading article summed up the May experience with the words, 'we can make whatever change we desire if we go the right way to work. The right way is the voting way'. – May 20th, 1926. Mr. Wheatley summed up the situation much more correctly when he said, 'The real tragedy was that in the hour of trial the Labour Movement was deserted by those in whom it had placed the greatest trust'.

The General Council of the Trades Union Congress followed the lead of the Baldwin Government, which after raiding Arcos institutions in London severed diplomatic relations with the Soviet Union. The general council severed its relations with the Russian trades unions because of the severe criticism and exposure the Russian trade union leaders had made of the general council's betrayal of the General Strike.

Now came the opportune moment for the Labour Party Executive to apply to the full its Liverpool Conference resolutions for the expulsion of the communists from the Labour Party. They and the trades union bureaucracy attacked all along the line. Union after union prohibited the communists and the supporters of the Minority Movement from holding any official position inside the unions and for the union branches and organizations to send delegates to conferences called by the Communist Party and the Minority Movement. They went further and prohibited the reading of correspondence from these organizations.

But the resistance was strong. Through its support of the miners the Communist Party recruited considerably. Its members increased to approximately 12,000 members. Arthur Horner was elected to the executive of the South Wales Miners' Federation. The Fife Miners' Association Executive passed into the hands of the communists and a number of leading positions were won in the Lanarkshire Miners' Association. The number of delegates to the Trades Union Congress had increased. A left wing workers' movement was organized of groups inside the Labour Party and the Independent Labour Party. At the Eighth Congress of the Communist Party it was reported that 'Not less than 28 different organizations have sent resolutions to the Margate conference of the Labour Party calling for the rescinding of the Liverpool decisions. Eleven local labour parties have been disaffiliated by the Labour Party Executive. There are approximately 150 groups and factions in the Labour Party. Forty-eigh labour parties have endorsed the Left wing programme.'

It was no easy matter therefore to defeat these forces and the course of events after the miners' strike did no make it easier. The General Strike and the Miners' Strik had played an important role in international affairs They had held back the British Government's attack upo the Chinese Revolution. No sooner had the miners strike ended than the Government proceeded with a aggressive policy in China. The advance of the Chines National Army from Southern China northward ha cleared the whole basin of the Yangtse-Kiang of opposi tion. For the first time the basis of British imperialism i Shanghai itself was threatened.

In the last week in November, 1926, naval air rein forcements were sent and at Tientsin fourteen Kuomintan students were handed over to the Northern troops sta tioned there. In January, 1927, British marines fired o a demonstration at Hankow and a spontaneous rising o the workers the next day retaliated by occupying th British Concession.

The Communists took the lead in organizing the protes movement in Britain. They issued an appeal for 'Hand off China' committees. They drew up a manifesto callin attention to the war peril. This document was signe not only by leading communists but also by G. Hicks R. B. Walker, J. Maxton, A. J. Cook, and others.

Seventy 'Hands off China' committees were establishe and conducted a great deal of agitation, all of whic retarded the expulsion policy of the bureaucracy. Th *Sunday Worker* and *Lansbury's Weekly* assisted considerabl in this campaign and stiffened resistance to the expulsio policy.

So strong was this resistance that twenty-two labour parties were disaffiliated rather than operate the resolutions. As late as June, 1928, the South Wales Miners' Federation Conference voted by 823 to 735 to support Communist Party affiliation to the Labour Party. But the Labour Party leaders pursued their course relentlessly. Where the labour parties were expelled they established new ones from which communists were excluded.

Great resistance was also organized to the expulsion of the Minority Movement from the unions. In spite of the ban of the executives and the General Council of the Trades Union Congress, 884 delegates attended the Fifth Congress of the National Minority Movement in London during August, 1928. But the council also went ahead. They broke up the joint committee they had organized with the unemployed workers. They issued a document to the trades councils demanding their loyalty and prohibiting them from having anything whatever to do with the Minority Movement.

The document campaign of the general council could have been defeated. The largest trades councils, such as Glasgow, Sheffield, and Manchester, were opposed to it. But the Communist Party and the Minority Movement suddenly appealed to the Trades Councils to sign this document in the name of 'unity'. The workers could not understand this new alliance of the communists and the general council and their resistance was killed.

A similar blunder was made in the Communist Party's attitude to the disaffiliated labour parties. They were told to apply for reaffiliation which was not obtainable without throwing out the communists, the very cause of their disaffiliation. Instead of organizing this discontent and revolt, the Communist Party gave the disaffiliated parties the option of joining the Communist Party or returning to the Labour Party. Naturally with this desertion they returned to the Labour Party. The Communist Party became more and more isolated and its membership decreased.

With this complete triumph of the right wing of the Labour Movement and the bankruptcy of the leadership of the revolutionaries there was no possibility of organizing mass resistance to anything the Government wished to do. It pursued its course with a minimum of opposition, which at best was only verbal. It put through the 'Miners' Eight Hour Act' which increased the working hours from seven to eight per day. This was followed by the Trade Union Act of 1927 which took away rights held by the unions for fifty years. Political strikes were made illegal. Severe restrictions were placed upon picketing. Sympathetic strikes were restricted. The principle of contracting out of the political levy was changed to 'contracting in'. It cut off all unions connected with state administration from political affiliation to the Labour Party. But there was no fight made against the Bill. A few wordy protests, a threat to repeal it by the next Labour Government, and nothing more.

Trade union membership consequently declined. Distrust of the leaders ran through the whole movement. But no force proved itself capable of leading it to a new challenge. There was nothing for the unhappy workers to do but wait for a change in the situation with the hope that it would bring new possibilities to advance.

CHAPTER XIII

THE SECOND CAPITALIST OFFENSIVE

No event in the history of the British working class so terrified the leaders of the Labour Movement as did the General Strike of 1926. The cry 'Never again' which went up from many leaders after it became history came from hearts that felt they had escaped from a terrible calamity.

This attitude of leaders was the very opposite to that of the workers. The magnificent solidarity of millions of working men and woman inspired them. At one blow they had silenced the cynics and doubters who had scoffed at the idea of the possibility of the workers displaying such solidarity and determination. Who could say after this event, 'They will not respond'?

The betrayal of the General Strike stunned the workers. They had placed implicit faith in their leaders and their leaders had let them down. Many months had to elapse before they began to move forward again. The failure of the revolutionaries during these months of bitter disillusionment to organize their discontent left the old leaders a free hand once more to determine the form and policy of the advance.

The Labour Party's Parliamentary programme had been obscured by the great strike movement. After the end of the miners' strike it was once more popularized. The General Council of the Trade Union Congress developed its programme of industrial reconstruction in co-operation with the union smashers, Mond and

Londonderry. The capitalists themselves, having got the Labour Movement to its knees, determined to secure the utmost out of their victory by extending and intensifying rationalization in industry.

The common denominator of these programmes was – a concerted effort of *all classes* for the development of capitalism.

This may be denied. But the documents of the period still exist and can be referred to. More important than the documents is the history that has been made on the basis of these documents.

Of course the Labour Party retained its socialist 'aim'. It included also in its programme a number of anti-capitalist demands. At the same time it rejected the policy of achieving socialism by class struggle and insisted on the necessity of the workers collaborating with the classes socialism must and is destined to abolish. In its preamble to 'Labour and the Nation' which contains not one paragraph of analysis of the crisis of capitalism, it declared once more its belief that capitalism is continuously being reformed into socialism. The years since Mr. Webb had expounded this theory of the unconscious 'imbibing' of socialism at the Labour Party Conference in 1923 had brought no recognition of the crisis of capitalism. The leaders of Labour still proceeded on the assumption that unemployment would grow less, that trade would improve and social reform would resume its even way.

The programme exposed the class contrasts, denounced the crimes committed against the workers and outlined a policy of social amelioration, international co-operation through the League of Nations and Empire development. How the improvements in workers' wages and conditions were to be secured without developing the class war was not explained. But it was argued that trade would improve through 'increasing the spending power of the masses' and the more scientific organization of industry. They said:

> 'The course dictated by considerations of common sense and humanity, the Labour Party holds, is precisely the opposite from this suicidal rivalry in mutual degradation. It is not to curtail the purchasing power of the population of Great Britain, which offers to British producers what is overwhelmingly their most important market. It is to maintain and increase it by every means in our power. The time has, happily, passed when employers could venture with impunity to follow the primrose path of economies effected at the cost of the health and vigour of the human personnel, for whom alone the industrial system is worth maintaining. If, as their spokesmen allege, they are eager to increase industrial efficiency, they will be well advised to begin by setting their own house in order – to modernize their organization, improve their technique, eliminate waste, and apply more intelligently the resources which science has revealed. . . .'

This injunction to the employers to 'set *their* house in order' etc., can hardly be interpreted otherwise than giving a blessing to the rationalizing of capitalist industry.

The General Council of the Trades Union Congress were a little more explicit. They got the Trades Union Congress to adopt the resolution of the Geneva World Economic Conference of 1927.[1] This clearly endorses capitalist rationalization of industry. How the net result

[1] The Geneva Resolution: 'The Conference considers that one of the principal means of increasing output, improving the conditions of labour and reducing costs of production is to be found in the rational organization of production and distribution.
The Conference considers that such rationalization aims simultaneously –

would conform to the hopes expressed in the resolution and by the trade union leaders is nowhere explained. How the increase in capitalist mass production methods on a competitive basis would result in 'greater stability' was not explained. Experience has proved this to be impossible. The technical revolution that proceeds continually in capitalism is recognized even by the capitalists themselves to be one of the greatest factors in increasing unemployment.

Nevertheless, the General Council of the Trades Union Congress says in its report to the Bristol Trades Union Congress in 1931:

> 'The Trades Union Congress adheres to the view that rationalization properly and wisely instituted and controlled will tend to produce these results and it was in that belief that the Trade Union Congress representatives in the Melchett-T.U.C. discussions supported the introduction of rationalization as defined in the World Economic Conference Resolution.'

1. At securing the maximum efficiency of labour with the minimum of effort.
2. At facilitating by a reduction in the variety of patterns (where such variety offers no obvious advantage) the design, manufacture, use and replacement of standardized parts.
3. At avoiding waste of raw materials and power.
4. At simplifying the distribution of goods.
5. At avoiding in distribution unnecessary transport, burdensome financial charges, and the useless interposition of middlemen.

'Its judicious and constant application is calculated to secure: –

1. To the community greater stability and a higher standard in the conditions of life.
2. To the consumer lower prices and goods more carefully adapted to general requirements.
3. To the various classes of producers higher and steadier remuneration to be equitably distributed among them.

It must be applied with the care which is necessary in order, while at the same time continuing the process of rationalization, not to injure the legitimate interests of the workers; and suitable measures should be provided for cases where during the first stages of its realization it may result in loss of employment or more arduous work.'

After this affirmation of belief that rationalization would produce the results they anticipated the General Council went on to say:

> 'It is therefore plain that the support of the Trades Union Congress has been given to rationalization *only in so far as it produces those results.*'

'Heads I win and tails you lose,' said the General Council. If rationalization had fulfilled their hopes we would have been told 'There, we told you so.' When it failed to produce the results predicted they answered, 'In those circumstances we disapproved of rationalization.' In both cases however they had given the employers the signal to go ahead. At what particular stage the general council would be able to discover that their beliefs were false and intervene to stop rationalization nobody could tell. The general council itself offered no information on the subject.

But their efforts went much further. They co-operated with the National Confederation of Employers and the Federation of British Industries in the production of memoranda on the economic and financial situation and upon empire development in which they were committed to supporting departure from the gold standard, the raising of wholesale prices, stabilization of prices, the rationalization of industry, all of which are typical capitalist measures approved later by the 'National Government'. They wanted an expanding market for British goods. They wanted to develop the Empire. They wanted everything which good Liberals and many Tories wanted. How the working class was to achieve socialism thereby no one attempted to explain. They worked on the gradualist assumption that capitalism can be reformed into socialism and the necessary pre-requisite for this reform is the well-being of capitalism.

The effect of the General Strike on the Independent Labour Party was profound. A new division of the party began. MacDonald and his supporters came to the conclusion that there was no need for the continued existence of the I.L.P. The I.L.P. had felt the need for a radical change in its policy. MacDonald and his followers dropped their pretence of Left sympathies and having made their position secure in the Labour Party leading ranks turned on their colleagues and denounced them as 'easy-oosie asses'.

The I.L.P. then came under the complete control of Maxton and the Clyde group who intensified their campaign for 'Socialism in Our Time'. The means to this end they described as the 'Living Wage Policy'.

This policy was based upon the theory that the capitalists should adopt the policy of high wages as the means to prosperity. Competition between capitalists was passing away and a new era of international trusts and scientific invention would pave the way to socialism as the 'defects' of capitalism were slowly eliminated. The attention of the workers was directed to America, where we were told, its prosperity refuted the theories of Marx. For example, the *New Leader* of March 26th, 1926, had an article by Mr. Wellock entitled, 'America as a school for socialists' in which he said:

> 'America's present condition proves what many of us have long contended, that it is possible for a community to live at almost any standard of life it desires. It may

live at the level of 30s. a week, £3 or £5. Or it may commit suicide. America had decided to live at the £5 per week level, whereas Great Britain has decided to commit suicide.'

(According to recent reports from America suicide appears to be infectious.) Mr. Brailsford, then editor of the *New Leader*, also wrote an article entitled 'Ford versus Marx' in the October 1st issue of his paper in which he said:

'If this is capitalism, it is a variety which has discarded the fundamental principle upon which Marx based his prediction. The case against it is no longer that it makes poverty by its very success. The case against it is rather that it is an unchecked autocracy . . .' As Mr. Ford advanced from his $2.40 average to his $5 and $6 minimum so we can raise our £2 a week to a £4 a week civilization, when we make up our minds to do it. . . .'

The same journal said in the issue of October 15th, 1926:

'The age of competition is passing, and the future may well bring vast international cartels controlling the food we eat, the clothes we wear, the tools we work with, the wages we earn; cartels before whose might the power of States will pale into insignificance.'

But the talk of higher wages and the dreams of higher social forms of organization were not advanced to encourage the workers to struggle against the capitalists who were reducing wages, but as an alternative to the wicked class war. The utopia was to be attained through a socialist government. The I.L.P. and the Labour Party held the view that the State was something apart from classes, something whose 'proper function' was to hold the balance between the classes and gently lead them both to the New Jerusalem to the tinkling of pastoral bells.

The idea that the State is the instrument of a class for maintaining its collective rule over the classes below it, however it may disguise its armour in democratic forms, was rejected by them. The General Strike had taught them nothing. Although class had confronted class and the State had stripped itself of its democratic disguises, although it had displayed its repressive powers quite nakedly against the class which challenged it, they continued to deplore the class struggle and moralized about the wrong distribution of wealth.

The I.L.P. placed on the agenda of the Labour Party Conference of 1927 the following resolution which typified their idealistic notions on the coming of socialism:

> 'This Conference declares that it is neither the object nor the duty of a Labour Government to administer the affairs of the nation in the interests of capitalism. It is of the opinion that the next Labour Administration, whatever the state of the parties in the House of Commons should introduce measures of real Socialist construction, particularly in the direction of securing an equitable Redistribution of the National Income; the reorganization of industry so as to obtain a living wage based on a decent standard for all workers; and the nationalization of the key industries.'

This was supported too by the group connected with *Lansbury's Weekly*. Some went further and published in this journal another programme which demanded the 'reconstruction of the State on socialist lines'. In this programme the Government remained a Parliamentary government but the writers said, 'It must throw over the convention of the alternation of parties . . . Labour's slogan must be, 'Get Power and Keep It. No more of the Ins and Outs'. It declared for the abolition of the House of Lords and said it must be abolished by the creation of a sufficient number of peers to vote and carry the decision to wipe out the House of Lords.

'Then,' it said, 'the Socialist government must proceed to the socialization of the banks, power, transport and land.' In place of Tariff Reform and Free Trade the government must establish the State control of foreign trade. These measures had to be accompanied by a social programme of improvement in wages, hours, housing, education, etc. It proposed further to grant Dominion Status to all parts of the Empire. Its international policy had to be that of remaining within the League of Nations to 'defend the rights of oppressed nationalities, disarmament by agreement and the settlement of international differences by arbitration'.

After the publication of this programme very little was said about it.

Thus the right wing of the Labour Movement, in complete control of all positions of power in the trade unions and the Labour Party, was able to pursue its course of collaboration with the capitalists unchecked. The I.L.P.'s campaign for the 'Living Wage' under the banner of 'Socialism in our Time' was not a challenge but an exhortation – a canalizing of discontent.

In the latter part of 1928, A. J. Cook, the Miners' leader, and J. Maxton, the chairman of the I.L.P., started a campaign for a socialist revival. This campaign contained much criticism both of the leaders of the Labour Movement and its programme. Great meetings were organized in many parts of the country. These meetings helped to reinvigorate the workers but were quite ineffective in altering the course of the Labour Party.

But an important change took place in the outlook and policy of the Communist Party and the Minority Movement. Up to this time, although the communists were organized in an independent party, they functioned mainly as a Left Wing of the Labour Party. Whilst conducting an independent propaganda for its revolutionary programme its main fight was against the 'Liberalizing of the Labour Party' and aimed at the transformation of the Labour Party from within.

This contradictory position was possible and largely due to the peculiar structure and nature of the Labour Party. The Labour Party began as a federation of trade unions and parties. Sooner or later it had to become one party. Immediately the communists formed an independent party, challenging the Labour Party leaders on fundamental questions of policy, the latter determined to use their overwhelmingly strong position to centralize their forces and to break the power of communism in its early stages of development. Had the grouping of the communists taken some other form than that of an independent party, claiming all the rights and assuming all the responsibilities of independence, it is extremely doubtful whether the expulsions of revolutionaries from the Labour Party would have been attempted.

Nevertheless, the Labour Party's refusal to accept the affiliation of the Communist Party did not make any fundamental change in the policy of the Communist

Party. The demand for the affiliation to the Labour Party became a part of the 'united front' tactic.

The first stages of the history of the Communist International, of which the Communist Party of Great Britain is a part, was a direct struggle to win the masses away from the Social Democratic leaders of the Second International. This was based upon the great mass revolutionary movement that swept across Europe after the Russian Revolution. The final aim was that of a single Workers' International of revolutionary class struggle against capitalism, carrying on the traditions and fulfilling the aims of the First International.

When the revolutionary tide turned and the Second International was re-establishing itself new tactics had to be adopted. These new tactics took the form of the 'united front' in which the communist parties, whilst recognizing the fundamental differences of aim and programme from those of the Second International and openly stating these differences, were prepared to organize common action with the Social Democrats for immediate aims upon which both could agree. This was considered possible because the Communists were convinced that in the process of the struggle their aims and policy would prove to be correct and the workers would finally follow them and not the Social Democrats.

Hence, although the Communist Party in Britain was refused admission to the Labour Party, both individually and collectively, the Communist Party continued to march alongside the Labour Party in opposition to the Tory and Liberal Parties and succeeded in winning considerable support. Its prestige after the General Strike and the Miners' Strike was high. Had it organized the disaffiliated Labour Parties on the basis of a workers' programme of action instead of impudently demanding that the disaffiliated Parties either join the Communist Party or return to the Labour Party; had it organized the revolt of the trades councils against the 'document' of the General Council of the Trades Union Congress into an independent federation of trade councils, the possibility of harnessing the mass disgust with the General Council's betrayal of the General Strike would have been within its grasp. This it failed to do and steadily its isolation increased and its membership declined. It thus proved to be opposed to transforming the Labour Party from within and incapable of organizing its friends who had supported it.

When, therefore, in 1929 it adopted what became known as the 'New Line', three years too late to be effective its isolation was increased. It declared that:

> 'Under no circumstances can the present situation be compared with the situation as it existed in 1918–1920, when Lenin insisted on supporting the Labour Party and pushing it into power. In 1918–1920, a Labour Party Government could have played the part of the Kerensky Government with all its vacillations. Nor can the present situation be compared with that of 1922–23, when the Labour Party had in its programme demands which were sharply resisted by the capitalist class (the capital levy, unemployment, Russia). No comparison can be made with the situation in 1924 when the Government was forced to resign on two objectively revolutionary issues. A Labour Government at the present juncture will be from the outset an obvious instrument for attacking the workers. The experience of the MacDonald Government, the betrayal of the

General Strike and the Miners' fight, the changed attitude of the Labour Party leaders towards the question of war and relations with the U.S.S.R., China, India, and Egypt, their changed attitude on the principal domestic questions (rationalization, the anti-Trade Union Bill, industrial peace), all this renders it necessary for the British Communist Party to come out more boldly and more clearly as an independent political party, to change its attitude towards the Labour Party and the Labour Government and consequently to replace the slogan of the Labour Government by the slogan of the Revolutionary Workers' Government.'[1]

In an earlier part of the same resolution it spoke of the 'imperative necessity to take advantage of the increasing swing to the left of the masses'. As already shown, however, it did not know how to take advantage of the 'leftward moving workers' and had driven them away from the Communist Party. This was not recognized and consequently it was left high and dry on the rocks of its own miscalculations. The Communist Party turned away from the Labour Party when the masses were returning to it.

On the strength of this analysis of the situation, which left out of account the effect of the class struggle upon the workers in the Labour Party, the Communist Party prepared a new programme upon which it fought the election of 1929.

Contrary to the Labour Party it laid down as the prerequisite for socialism the necessity of the Dictatorship of the Proletariat. Instead of a Parliamentary Government

[1] *Communist Policy in Britain*, p. 194.

it set before the workers the need to prepare for a 'Revolutionary Workers' Government, exercising a working-class dictatorship and operating a real workers' democracy' through workers' councils composed of delegates from the factories and the mass organizations of the workers.

It outlined the programme of a Revolutionary Workers' Government. It said that such a Government of the Workers would 'declare this country to be a Workers' Socialist Republic, consolidate its power and safeguard it from counter revolution and external capitalist attack by organizing its own revolutionary workers' army, navy and air force. It would nationalize the banks, the land, the mines, the railways, land and sea transport, electrical industries, broadcasting stations, engineering and shipbuilding industries, post and telegraph, chemical, cotton and woollen industries, flour milling, boot and shoe industries and building materials, all of which are ripe for running as national industries, unitedly owned and controlled by the workers'.

These fundamental measures were to be the foundation for the planned development of the economy of the country and for an extensive development of social services, improvement of working conditions throughout industry, higher education for the masses and the elimination of the exploitation of man by man.

Its foreign policy had to be equally drastic and far reaching. The Revolutionary Workers' Government must declare the independence of every country hitherto ruled and controlled by British imperialism and offer them friendly assistance to maintain their independence and develop in the direction of Workers and Peasants' Republics. It would repudiate the League of Nations, publish all secret treaties, support the programme of the

Soviet Union for simultaneous international disarmament as the means to end war, would establish immediate unity and federation with the Soviet Union and thus prove itself to be the friend of the oppressed workers and peasants of the whole world.

By the time of the General Election of 1929 the actions of the Baldwin Government had roused the deepest feelings of the workers against it. All the anger that they felt against the anti-Trade Union Act, the Miners' Eight Hour Act and the severance of relations with the Soviet Union found expression in a tremendous increase of the Labour vote, 8,362,394 votes were registered for the Labour Party and two hundred and eighty nine Labour candidates were returned to Parliament.

The Labour Party became thereby the largest party in the House of Commons, but it had not a majority over all other parties. The Labour Movement was jubilant and not one of its leaders realized how near was a new rapid development of the crisis of capitalism. The second Labour Government was formed with Mr. MacDonald once more at its head.

It began again with many promises of the good things which were to come to the workers. 'Among the first tasks of the Labour Party,' said the *Labour and the Nation* programme, 'will be the repeal of the cynical measures of class legislation by which the Conservatives have sought to cripple the strength of trades unionism both on the industrial field and on the political fields' (p. 16) – There were two years of Labour Government. The Trade Union Act is still on the statute book.

'The disastrous act by which the Tory Government added an hour to the working day must be at once repealed' – It was not repealed and only after tremendous pressure from outside parliament were the miners able to get a seven and a half hour day.

'Bills will be laid before you for amending and consolidating the existing factory legislation, and for giving effect to the obligations entered into in Washington in 1919' (King's speech, July 1929). – There has been no new factory legislation and the Washington Convention is still unratified.

Once more the Labour Government found itself engrossed in the task of administering capitalism in the midst of increasing difficulties. Instead of reforming capitalism into socialism it became increasingly engaged in defending capitalism against the measures it was committed by its programme to support. It viewed the unemployment situation through optimistic spectacles. Still holding to the capitalist view of the crisis it felt sure that 'good trade' was just round the corner. There were at the time of the General Election in 1929, one million and a quarter registered unemployed. There was then no talk of 'economic blizzards' or of a crisis in America. Indeed Mr. Tillett told the Trades Union Congress to gaze on America's 'ever expanding prosperity'. When the Labour Party Conference met in October, 1929, there were many protests concerning the increasing volume of unemployment.

Mr. J. H. Thomas called forth cheers with his reply. 'I am confident,' he said, 'that when February comes the unemployment figures will be far different and better than the figures during the late government.' The conference was assured by Mr. Morrison that Mr. Ramsay MacDonald was fulfilling the role of 'political leader of the nation'. 'He will live in history,' said Mr. Morrison, 'not only as the first Labour Prime Minister but as a statesman and servant of the people of the first order.' With these assurances the Government and the Labour Movement went blindly on towards calamity.

But they had no remedies other than the capitalist remedies, all of which they excused on the grounds of being a minority government. Nobody seemed ready to ask the question, 'Why continue in a position where we have to do everything which we don't want to do?' The fact was, that having accepted the policy of gradualism, they were committed to getting capitalism on to its feet before they could give any attention to their programme of promises. Because the demands they had set forth in their programme on behalf of the workers were in flat contradiction to the requirements and needs of capitalism, their own theories forced them to take sides with the capitalists against the workers.

They had declared in their programme that 'The Labour Party holds that to attempt to cheapen production by attacking the standard of life of the workers of the nation is not only socially disastrous, but highly injurious to the economic prosperity of the whole community.' But the Labour Government took a leading part in the reducing of the wages of the cotton operatives by 7½ per cent, the Woollen Workers by 9½ per cent and the Jute Workers by 4 per cent. It applied the Tory Trade Union Act to strikers, and passed the Anomalies Bill against the Unemployed.

The imperialist policy of the Government was indistinguishable from that of its predecessor, except that it was more violent. One of its first actions was to endorse the arrest of the thirty-one workers' leaders in India on a charge of 'Conspiracy against the King', and the trial of the arrested men at Meerut. It acquiesced to the additional arrest of H. L. Hutchinson by the Indian government, and to the spending of £750,000 on the prosecution. It refused a jury. It refused bail to the prisoners. The trial continued for the whole two years of the Labour Government. To-day the Labour Party denounces the trial as a 'judicial scandal' and is demanding the release of the prisoners who have been given sentences ranging from three years to imprisonment for life' (later considerably modified).

By August, 1930, the gaols of India were full. Not less than 20,000 Indian Nationalists were imprisoned. Uprisings were suppressed by military forces. Every principal city of India has been the scene of vast demonstrations and conflicts with police and troops. Martial law has been put in operation on many occasions and the death roll amounts to hundreds.

Uprisings in Egypt were similarly suppressed. 'A demonstration strike in Alexandria against the shooting of demonstrators was suppressed by force. Fifteen civilians were killed and sixty wounded by bullets and 160 injured.'[1] Big casualty lists also accompanied the establishment of 'law and order' in Palestine and Nigeria.

But neither the violence of the imperial forces nor the wage cutting at home prevented the Labour Government from being embroiled in the crisis they had not foreseen. Instead of finding the corner round which 'good trade' is supposed to be hidden unemployment continued to grow rapidly. They appointed Sir George May and a committee to examine the 'national finances'. The report of this committee appeared at a critical moment in the midst of the credit crisis started by the failure of the Austrian Credit Anstalt. This report declared that the budgetary

[1] *The Times*, July 16th, 1930.

position was such that unless drastic measures were immediately taken there would be a Budget deficit of £120,000,000 for the year 1932–33.

All through 1931 the economic situation was going from bad to worse. In the second quarter of 1931 the output of British industry had fallen to 92.5 per cent of its 1924 level, which must be remembered was itself ten per cent below the level of 1913. The iron and steel index was 63 per cent, textiles 75 per cent and coal 80 per cent of the 1924 level. The volume of exports had fallen to 66 per cent of 1924. Prices of industrial materials were well below the 1913 level. In the distributive trades the trusts reported a decline in turnover of 4.2 per cent in the year.

But stupid optimism prevailed. 'At last a real revival of trade is in sight . . .' said the *Daily Herald* of April 10th, 1931. 'Many references have been made to a possible improvement in trade. Now there are definite signs of recovery.'

When the financial crisis developed the same kind of bluff was still carried on. On July 20th, 1931, the *Daily Herald* carried a leading article entitled 'The Turn of the Tide'. It said 'Never since the fateful days of August, 1914, when war or peace hung in the balance, was this country nearer to crash and calamity than during the last seven days . . . When the full history is written, people will be amazed to learn how near we were to the edge of the precipice . . .' A few days later the same paper refuted the 'mischievous and grotesque rumours' of credits from abroad.[1] On August 1st Britain was granted £50,000,000 credits by France and the U.S.A.

The final days of the Labour Government were days of

[1] July 29th, 1931.

the greatest confusion, contradictory rumours, accusations and counter accusations. All agreed that the Budget must be balanced. How? According to the General Councils Report to the Trades Union Congress on September 9th, 1931, the Cabinet had appointed a Committee which had been preparing schemes for meeting the emergency. It consisted of Mr. MacDonald, Mr. Snowden, Mr. Henderson, Mr. Graham and Mr. J. H. Thomas.

This Committee met the General Council and reported on the proposed economies. 'These economies,' says the report[1] included raising of unemployment contributions, restricting insurance benefits to twenty-six weeks in the year, reducing the pay of teachers, police and members of the armed forces, reducing the expenditure on roads and grants under the Unemployment Grants Scheme, and one or two other items including the reduction of salaries of Cabinet Ministers, Judges and Members of Parliament.'

To these 'economies', which were contrary to all the promises of the Labour Party, was added the demand for ten per cent cut in unemployment benefits. This split the Cabinet. MacDonald dissolved the Government. He, Mr. Snowden and Mr. J. H. Thomas took with them a handful of supporters from the Parliamentary Labour Party and formed a 'National Government' – a new coalition government with the Tories and Liberals. The majority of the Parliamentary Labour Party refused to follow.

A panic election was quickly organized by the 'National Government'. Visions of an inflation panic were held before the people who were told that their savings were

[1] Sixty-Third Annual Report of the T.U.C., p. 513.

in danger. Disasters of stupendous dimensions were foreshadowed for the country. Only a 'National Government' could prevent chaos.

MacDonald returned at the head of the Tory, Liberal, ex-Labour combination. The Tories were in a great majority. Labour was heavily defeated. But the crisis deepened.

CHAPTER XIV

PERSPECTIVES AND CONCLUSIONS

THE crisis of 1931 decisively changed the relations of all parties. It brought down the Labour Government; the Labour Party lost leaders who had controlled its politics for thirty years; it split the Liberal Party once more; it produced a new Coalition in the form of the 'National Government' which included Tory, Liberal and 'National Labour'; the Labour Party was thrust into opposition. Instead of a resumption of the old two party system Britain was brought nearer to a confrontation of parties on class lines.

But the Parliamentary groupings were only the outward form of inner political changes still more profound. With the advent of the National Government, Britain ceased to be a 'Free Trade' country. 'Free Trade' belongs essentially to the period when Britain was the workshop of the world.

The modern tariff policy belongs to the period of monopoly capitalism, that is, imperialism. It is a weapon of economic warfare between competing monopolists. It was only to be expected that the young rising imperialist powers should adopt the tariff policy first and that the oldest capitalist power which had established its monopoly under the banner of 'Free Trade' should be the last to adopt the policy of tariffs.

Nor did it stop at that. The 'National' Government supplemented its tariff war with a currency war. It pushed the £ off the Gold Standard in order to secure advantages for the export trade.

Later still the Government adopted the quota system, that is, the determination of foreign imports by quantity, instead of trusting to the operation of the deterrent of the tariff. This was considered to be more effective in limiting the importation of foreign goods.

Such measures are the economics of desperation. Britain cannot act in isolation. Other countries have pursued a similar policy. The net result is the further stagnation of international trade.[1] The measures enumerated can have no other result than that of intensifying the international competition for the contracting world market.

The internal result cannot have a mitigating effect upon the international situation. For a time, and a short time at that, it may lead to an apparent improvement whilst there is going on a process of saturation of the home market by 'British produced' goods by the exclusion of foreign goods.

Once that point has been reached, then the need for further expansion of foreign trade will accentuate the international competition and inevitably intensify the crisis conditions with less chance of mitigation.

[1] According to 'Labour Research', February, 1933, World Trade (Exports) declined by 62 per cent, compared with the year 1929.

The industrial production of leading imperialist countries moved as follows (1929 = 100):

	1930	1931	*3rd quarter* 1932
World (excluding U.S.S.R.)	85	72	58
U.S.A.	81	69	52
Britain	92	83	78
Germany	82	69	53
France	101	89	66
Poland	82	69	56

The Industrial Production of the U.S.S.R. moved as follows (1928 = 100).

1929	1930	1931	1932
124.2	156.3	189.3	196.1

The rapidity with which the currency war is developing into world wide inflation shows how rapidly capitalism is moving from one crisis to another and how each crisis intensifies the general chaos.

The average capitalist politician and a considerable number of Labour politicians too, try to explain the crisis as a 'distribution crisis'. They thus become involved in all the talk about 'increasing the spending power of the masses', 'removing tariff barriers', demanding 'cheap money', 'control of price', 'inflation of the currency', all of which are the most superficial proposals which leave the root cause of the crisis untouched, indeed intensify it if attempted.

Yet the cause of the crisis is not a mystery. The nature, cause and inevitability of the crisis which have grown with cumulative effect and increasingly devastating consequences to the vast majority of mankind are well known.

In the introduction to the *Critique of Political Economy* Marx says:

> 'At a certain stage of their development, the material forces of production in society come in conflict with the existing relations of production, or – what is but a legal expression for the same thing – with the property relations within which they have been at work before. From forms of development of the forces of production these relations turn into their fetters. Then comes the period of social revolution.'

But the last thing on earth which the capitalists will discuss is the removal of those fetters. They stand before the world with hands outstretched babbling about the 'curse of plenty!' Mr. Winston Churchill is a striking example of the complete helplessness of the modern capitalists and their spokesmen. In his Romanes lecture in 1930 he said:

> 'The root problem of modern world economics was the strange discordance between the consuming and producing power. Who would have thought that cheap and abundant supplies of all the basic commodities should find the science of civilization of the world unable to use them? Had all the triumphs of research and organization bequeathed to us only a new punishment – the curse of plenty?'

Thus the brilliant minds of capitalism stand paralysed before the problems created by capitalism. But not so the Marxist revolutionaries. Engels wrote as far back as 1892 in *Socialism Utopian and Scientific.*

> 'The whole mechanism of the capitalist mode of production breaks down under the pressure of the productive forces of its own creation. It is no longer able to turn all this mass of means of production into capital. They lie fallow, and for that very reason the industrial reserve army must also lie fallow. Means of production, means of subsistence, available labourers, all the elements of production and general wealth, are present in abundance. But 'abundance becomes the source of distress and want' (Fourier) because it is the very thing that prevents the transformation of the means of production and subsistence into capital.'

Having diagnosed the cause Engels did not stand bewildered but went on to point out the solution. He continued:

> 'The solution can only consist in the practical recognition of the social nature of the modern forces of

production, and therefore in the harmonizing the modes of production, appropriation and exchange with the social character of the means of production. And this can only come about by society openly and directly taking possession of the productive forces which have outgrown all control except that of society as a whole. The social character of the means of production and of the products to-day reacts against the producers, periodically disrupts all production and exchange, acts only like a law of Nature working blindly, forcibly, destructively. But with the taking over by society of the productive forces, the social character of the means of production and of the products will be utilized by the producers with a perfect understanding of its nature, and instead of being a source of disturbance and collapse, will become the most powerful lever of production itself.'

Precisely because the Bolshevik revolution adopted the methods indicated by Marx and Engels, the Soviet Union is the one country in the world without unemployment, without a production crisis and is unlikely to have one whilst the rest of the world rushes into deeper and deeper chaos.

The principal issue of this age therefore is neither tariffs nor inflation, neither embargoes nor debts, nor quotas, nor shorter hours, nor wage rates. These are only by-products of the principal issue – the retention of the private ownership of the means of production. This property question dominates all questions. Social ownership of the means of life must supersede private ownership. The longer private property relations continue the more the struggle for their retention drives towards Fascism in the internal life of capitalist countries and towards a new imperialist world war.

This applies as much to this country as to other capitalist countries. The 'National Government' is not an accidental event. The first Coalition Government was the product of the first stage of the crisis of imperialism which had burst in the flames of war. The second Coalition Government was the product of the situation at the end of the war when the revolutionary offensive of the working class drove the defenders of private property into a corner. The third Coalition – the 'National Government' – is the product of a still more serious stage of the crisis.

Each coalition has had different features. The first embraced the Labour Movement. The second was against the Labour Movement on the offensive. The period in between the second and third Coalition Governments was marked by incessant efforts, sometimes by cunning manœuvres such as the formation of minority Labour governments which were hidden forms of Coalition, and at other times by direct conflict, to secure the complete co-operation and subordination of the organized Labour Movement for the preservation of private property. They failed with the collapse of the second Labour Government. The third Coalition is organized against the Labour Movement, which shrank from further sacrificing the working class and lower middle class on the altar of private property.

The vacillations and contradictions of the Labour Movement throughout this period, and indeed prior to it, are the direct sequel to the attempt of its leaders to control a class movement with the policy of what is now dying capitalist liberalism. There is and can be no other explanation of the remarkable record we have surveyed in these pages.

At one moment they called for Workers' and Soldiers'

Councils, the institutions of revolution. They shrank from this 'too great' loyalty to the revolution and staked their all upon Parliamentary democracy. They threatened a general strike to stop a war and were thrilled by success, only once more to show fear of its implications. They were overtaken by 'Black Friday' and sectional defeats. They called a general strike, betrayed it and many went so far as to repudiate it. They joined with capitalist politicians in forecasting 'prosperity round the corner', and built a policy of the 'inevitability of gradualism' upon it. The prosperity did not come. In its stead came calamity. Instead of gradual reforms came the avalanche of capitalist attack upon all reforms – wage cuts, cuts in unemployment pay, cuts in the pay of teachers, soldiers, sailors.

They saw nothing in the decay of the Liberal Party except an opportunity to replace it with a Liberal-Labour Party.

But the disintegration of the Liberal Party is as significant as the failure of liberal politics within the Labour Party. All attempts to rebuild the Liberal Party have failed and must fail. It has no future other than that of a temporary auxiliary of the Tory Party pending the time when British capitalism decides to have single party rule. The growth of finance capitalism at the head of which stand the great banks, absorbing the rentiers and capitalists of all kinds leaves no room for alternating capitalist parties. The centralization of economic power disposes of the need for capitalist parties expressing rival interests, and as the crisis deepens the domination of a single party in charge of the capitalist state, as in the case of Germany and Italy, will inevitably become the supreme question before the capitalist class.

The interests upon which the Labour Party, the trade unions and the Co-operative Societies have been built cannot be absorbed by the banks nor represented by any capitalist party. The antagonism of their interests and those of the capitalists are too fundamental. It is precisely because of this fact that with the growth of the fascist idea of single party Government also grows the idea of smashing the Labour Movement and transforming the working class into a helot class.

It is impossible to deny that these developments have been accompanied by an intensification of the class war. For such a recognition it is only necessary to recall from the survey of the struggle made in these pages – the appearance of the Emergency Powers Act in 1919, the Organization for the Maintenance of Supplies, the numerous demonstrations of military and naval forces in disputes, the passing of the anti-Trade Union Act, the new Police Bill and its militarization of the police force, the great strikes of recent years, the General Strike, the big demonstrations of unemployed Workers, the Invergordon revolt, in short the whole drama of the struggle since the war.

The welcome given by many members of the ruling class to the triumph of Hitlerism in Germany, the actual beginning of open fascists' organizations, the numerous fights between Fascists and anti-fascist forces, the press campaign for the 'Big Man' and its popularization of Mussolini demonstrate that the defenders of private property are turning to fascism. Mr. Baldwin declared in his Glasgow speech of June 22nd, 1933, that 'Britain will not stand for a dictatorship from the right or from the left.' So said Hindenburg of Germany and a few months later became the President of Hitler's Fascist Republic.

The growth of Fascism in this country does not depend upon the faith of Mr. Baldwin but upon the rapidity with which the world economic crisis develops and the chaos which ensues. Capitalist politicians, including Mr. Baldwin, will find all the reasons necessary for Fascism the more imperative becomes the demand for the abolition of the private ownership of the means of production. Behind all the bland assurances of to-day is the determination of the propertied classes to stand firmly for the sacred rights of private property – Rent, Interest and Profits.

Once this fact is recognized it is crystal clear that the change from private property relations of capitalism to socialism depends primarily upon the actions of the working class – the propertyless class. It is necessary therefore in concluding our survey to ask – how stands the working-class movement in relation to this fundamental task of emancipating the people of this country from the thraldom of private property relations?

The crisis of 1931, which brought down the Labour Government, did not change the relative positions of the Labour Party and trade unions to the communists. The Communist Party made a serious miscalculation after the General Election of that year. It argued that the Labour Party was in collapse. It failed to distinguish between the collapse of leaders and the collapse of a movement. Seven million votes in a panic election, a few hours after three of its leaders of thirty years standing had split from the party, cannot be truthfully described as the sign of a party in collapse.

It is an outstanding fact of the Labour Party's history that it has withstood its internal crisis in a remarkable manner. Possibly this was due to the bad tactics pursued by the Communist Party and MacDonald in the differing critical situations with which they were specially concerned, but the fact is, that the Party remains intact. The Communist Party continues to diffuse influence but makes no headway in organizing an alternative movement to that of the Labour Party. It continues to complain of its isolation from the masses.[1]

Nevertheless the Labour Party has felt the effect of the discrediting of its policy of 'gradualism'. Immediately after the fall of the Labour Government there arose an insistent demand that the next Labour Government should immediately proceed with fundamental socialist measures rather than make further attempts to 'tinker' with capitalism. A new differentiation began to show itself in the leaders of the Party.

Sir Stafford Cripps, Sir Charles Trevelyan, Mr. George Lansbury and Major Attlee, all of whom had been members of the Labour Government, became outspoken in their denunciations of 'gradualism' and insistent upon the necessity of a Labour government being a socialist government, applying immediately on its assumption of office, the fundamental measures of socialism. A number of trade union leaders also demanded such a policy. At the Labour Party Conference in 1932 those who stood for this drastic change of policy received a great reception from the Conference and it was obvious that the mass of the movement was more than ready for the change.

Immediately prior to this conference the Socialist

[1] '. . . In face of the rapid growth of the capitalist crisis and the increasing fighting spirit of the workers, the Party is still lagging behind and is dangerously isolated from the mass struggles of the workers . . .

'Even when the recruits join the Party from mass recruiting meetings, no serious effort is made to retain them. This is shown in the big fluctuation of membership throughout the Party. . . .' – Resolutions Twelfth Congress of the Communist Party, 1932, p. 20.

League was formed. This organization was composed at first mainly of that section of the Independent Labour Party which had refused to follow the lead for disaffiliation from the Labour Party. This split of the I.L.P. had occurred earlier in the year. It was the culmination of the process begun when MacDonald and Snowden with their supporters left the I.L.P. and the party passed into the control of the supporters of Mr. J. Maxton. This change led to an increasing insistence upon independent I.L.P. voting on the questions before the House of Commons. The refusal of the I.L.P. to accept the discipline of the Parliamentary Labour Party led to the decision to disaffiliate from the Labour Party. After this decision the I.L.P. declared itself to be a Marxist Party, although it had previously repudiated Marxism. From this moment it came closer to the Communist Party but has striven to maintain its independence. It must eventually be absorbed by one or other of these parties. Already it is in process of disintegration and facing another split. It cannot hope to build an alternative Parliamentary Party to the Labour Party. It cannot supersede the Communist Party. It lacks cohesion and the international support of the communists. Struggling to justify a centrist position it is ineffective in winning communists to its ranks and equally ineffective in influencing or winning forces from the Labour Party.

Since its formation at the Leicester Conference the Socialist League has consequently become the focus of the new demand for a change of policy in the Labour Party. It has now passed beyond the stage of repeating the history of the I.L.P. At its conference in 1933 it decided against any attempt to be a parallel organization to that of the Labour Party. It decided to work as an integral part of that Party expressing the revolutionary socialist opinions and policy within it and striving to win the rest of the Labour Party to its point of view.

Its programme is very similar at this stage to that of the *Lansbury Weekly* group (see p. 248) demanding that the next Labour Government shall by use of an Emergency Powers Act take all the necessary powers to remove the obstacles standing in the way of the immediate application of fundamental socialist measures such as the socialization of the banks, industry and land.[1] This programme is strictly limited to the tasks before the next Labour Government. Apart from its declarations against fascism and war it has not developed its programme. Nevertheless this question of the tasks of the next Labour Government represents the form in which the revolt against gradualism has expressed itself in the Labour Movement as a whole up to the time of the Fascist Revolution in Germany.

The coming of the fascist dictatorship in Germany

[1] 'Socialist League Programme of Action'. Adopted at the Annual Conference, 1933.
1. The immediate introduction by a Labour Government of an Emergency Powers Act, giving it authority at once to take over or regulate the financial machine, and to take any measures that the situation may require for the immediate control or socialization of industry and for safeguarding the supply of food and other necessaries.
2. The securing of guarantees for the abolition of the House of Lords prior to taking office.
3. As part of the Labour Programme at the next election the demand for power to operate a policy of planned economic development, based on the socialization of finance (including the Joint Stock Banks), land, mines, power, transport, iron and steel, cotton, and the control of foreign trade.
4. The necessity for self-government in industry as an essential part of Socialist Reconstruction, and the preparation of plans giving concrete expression to this in industries or services nationalized by a Labour Government.
5. The restriction of compensation for nationalized property to income allowances for a limited period of years only, and the rapid elimination of

made this policy discussion more important then ever before and has accentuated the differences within the Labour Party. Unquestionably, the whole working-class movement has become alarmed at the danger of Fascism. At all conferences and public meetings, whether of the Labour Party, of the trade unions or the Co-operative Societies and Guilds, protests against the destruction of the working-class organizations of Germany are being made. These protests are being accompanied by declarations of belief in the democratic institutions of this country and the achievement of socialism through education and the vote.

At the recent conference of Co-operative Women a resolution was passed recognizing the spread of fascism in Britain and calling upon the workers to unite 'to defend their constitutional right to alter the social system by education and organization'. Mrs. Pavitt speaking on behalf of the central committee of the Co-operative Women's Guild said:

all charges arising from former private ownership of nationalized property by taxation dealing similarly with property generally.

6. Emergency action on Unemployment, to make effective the slogan 'Work or Maintenance' before the full results in relation to Employment of the Economic Plan and Socialization have been obtained. The following to be applied at once:

(*a*) The Government to take responsibility for providing and financing development through a programme which should include the building of at least one million houses, to replace slum and semi-slum dwellings within four years, to be let at rates within the workers' capacity to pay; by agricultural expansion; and by organizing the supply of other mass needs in this country and overseas.

(*b*) The adoption as a minimum of the T.U.C. scale for the unemployed on a non-contributory basis; the abolition of the Means Test and of the Anomalies Act and Regulations.

(*c*) The lowering of the Pensions age to 60, the raising of the rate and the institution of a non-contributory scheme.

(*d*) Raising the school age at once to 15 and thereafter to 16, with maintenance grants.

7. The granting of full civil rights to all State employees.

> 'We in this country have the finest democratic institutions in the world, and the reason why we find ourselves in the position which exists to-day is because we have not rightly used the powers we possess. Your power is your vote.'

Mr. Citrine speaking to the same Conference on behalf of the General Council of the T.U.C. said:

> 'Our great voluntary organizations are united in their resistance to dictatorship. Each is determined to preserve the democratic foundations which had fostered its growth.'

Other conferences and other speakers sound the same note. At the same time a number have gone further and taken exception to the declarations of Sir Stafford Cripps, who is in favour of the next Socialist government being empowered to use Emergency Powers to remove the obstacles to the introduction of socialism. These views are regarded as favouring dictatorship. Mr. H. B. Lees-Smith declared in the *Daily Herald* of June 26th, 1933:

> 'Let there be no mistake, if a dictatorship is ever established in this country it will be by our opponents and not ourselves.
> And any threat in that direction from us will be met by our opponents long before we have the opportunity to do anything ourselves. It is unfortunate therefore that the first talk about dictatorship should be coming from Labour ranks.'

Thus once more the voice of Liberalism with its assurances

to capitalism, is raised loudly in the Labour Movement against the call for socialism.

At the same time all proposals for a united front with working-class revolutionaries outside the Labour Party have been rejected. A new process of 'cleansing' has begun. Instructions have once more been sent out forbidding association with communists for any purpose. Instead of seizing the opportunity presented by the publication of the manifestos of the Second and the Communist Internationals regarding the necessity of united action on the part of all anti-fascist forces, the Labour Party answered with a Liberal Manifesto on the virtues of 'democracy', a widening of the division between itself and the communists. Thus is repeated the history of the German Social Democratic Party, despite the hammer blows of Hitler on the heads of social democrats and communists alike. Hitler demonstrated by deeds both the common origin of social democracy and communism and that socialism is a class question.

The working class of this country stands before the greatest crisis of its history. It has to decide whether it will fight for socialism and democracy or dissipate its energy in wordy warfare about democracy and lose both the democratic gains won in the course of its struggle and socialism too.

There can be no question for the socialist of the necessity to defend whatever democratic rights have been won. But the Labour Movement can only forget at its own peril that these rights have come from the class struggle. It may be that the defence of these rights expressed in the Parliamentary system will play the same role in the struggles ahead of the British working class as the demand for the Constituent Assembly in the history of the Russian

Revolution. But it will be fatal to socialism and the British working-class movement, if the defence of Parliamentary institutions becomes an end in itself. It is not the Parliamentary system that can solve the crisis of capitalism. That is the task of socialism. The race is not between democracy and fascism but between socialism and fascism.

Let us above all things be clear on this question.

It must not be forgotten that the holding of elections is determined by the class *in power*. If it deems that a 'state of emergency' exists and an election would interfere with its continued rule it can postpone an election indefinitely, as it did at the outbreak of war. To conduct an election in a crisis knowing that the victory of the opposition means the coming of socialism, *is equivalent to a voluntary surrender of capitalism to socialism.* Will the British capitalist class be so loyal to democratic forms and procedure as to make such a voluntary surrender?

Is the situation such that the Labour Movement can complacently proceed merely with election plans on the assumption that such an easy journey lies before it? The writer is of the opinion that such an attitude would be fatal.

Fascism does not wait for an 'indiscreet' utterance of some leader of the Labour Party or for election decisions. The forces out of which the fascist form of government evolve are already in power. The fascist developments in Britain have been rapidly maturing long before the present discussion in the Labour Party or the fall of the last Labour Government.

Fascism is inherent in the crisis of capitalism. The more desperate the position of capitalism the more determined becomes the will of the capitalists to sweep away every impediment to their domination and exploitation of the workers. To suggest that the present government of incipient fascism is likely to have much regard to democratic forms in order to conform to the election plans of the Labour Movement is absurd.

But the crisis of capitalism drives not only towards fascism in the internal life of the country, it drives also towards war internationally. No one to-day disputes the war danger. Armaments are increasing. The so-called disarmament conference can be written off as collapsed. Military budgets are being increased enormously. Every international conference reveals an increased tension between the Powers. These facts are acknowledged. Everybody knows that in the event of the outbreak of war the question of participation will not be submitted to a general election. On the contrary there will be an unqualified dictatorship with military and industrial conscription.

There is still another possibility latent in the situation. The 'National Government' may suddenly decide upon a general election because it considers that it would be again returned. Alternatively, because it considers it would be able to make a further split in the Labour Party forces for the purpose of creating a still wider coalition. It is the task of the Government in any society of which it is the custodian to secure the greatest possible mass support and to weaken, divide, and reduce to ineffectiveness the parties of any opposing social order. To rule out the possibility of such a development, therefore, is to blind oneself to the realities of the political struggle and to assume that all the MacDonalds, Snowdens, and Thomases have left the Labour Party – a consummation desired but not yet realized.

Nor can we dismiss the possibility of an election which would make the Labour Party again the largest party, but without an absolute majority over all others. Such a situation may even be deliberately staged with a view to rapidly discrediting Parliamentary politics, creating further discontent with Labour policy and securing the popular justification for fascist forms of government.

The whole question of the preservation of democratic rights as a means to socialism and the future of socialism itself against the advance of fascism and war, depend therefore upon the power of the organized working-class movement and the willingness of the leaders to use that power. If the whole strategy and tactics of the Labour Party turn upon pacifist protests and passive waiting for an election which may not come, then Fascism and War are certain winners in the political race. Just as the whole policy of reforming prosperous capitalism collapsed in the face of a capitalism which has ceased to be prosperous and cannot become prosperous, so the policy of waiting for the capitalist mind to become more Liberal and tolerant to socialism will collapse in the face of a capitalist class grown desperate and fascist.

The second collapse of Labour will be more disastrous than anything which has preceded it. 1931 proved that it was useless to dodge the fact that all the immediate programmes of social improvement, better social services, amelioration of unemployment, can no longer be attained by legislation unless preceded by fundamental socialist change – the socialization of the means of production. The collapse of 1931 still leaves time for its lessons to be assimilated before the second crisis becomes acute.

The second crisis now developing demands the most far-reaching changes in the life and activity of the whole

Labour Movement. From a purely defensive movement against the pressure of capitalism it must develop into an offensive for socialism. So long as it merely sounds the alarm and warns the people of the wrath to come it can give inspiration to nobody. It can thereby only increase doubts and fears and develop the feeling of the inevitability of defeat. A movement that attempts to live by apology, that merely defends the existing situation is half dead already. Defensive actions to-day must be regarded as skirmishes, important skirmishes truly, but skirmishes nevertheless in the major struggle for socialism.

The declarations and manifestations of capitalist bankruptcy must be received with joy and answered with the confident affirmation that the hour has struck for the working class to advance with its socialist solution of the crisis. Without this there can be no inspiration for the workers to fight, no call to youth to dare and dare again, no appeal to the masses to see in the advance to socialism their own emancipation. The difficulties of capitalism are Labour's opportunities to strike blows for Socialism, to advance to the decisive fight for Socialism.

This involves a complete change in the strategy of the movement from mere electioneering to that of a complete mobilization of all possible forces at its disposal for all forms of action. It involves a change in the tactics of the Labour Movement whereby every question of the daily struggle, whether it be in the defence of wages or for an increase of wages, whether it be against an encroachment on some democratic right or for some positive gain of this or that, becomes a means for the fulfilment of the greater strategy of the massing of the forces of the working class and all forces sympathetic to socialism, ready for the decisive struggle.

To shirk these facts is to ignore the entire history of the Labour Movement, to hand over the workers' organizations of the revolutionary working class to the forces of counter-revolutionary fascism. To face the facts boldly and proclaim them, would stamp out of the movement the deadly cynicism, the scepticism, the lack of faith which have eaten into its ranks with the repeated disappointments that have marked the years since the General Strike of 1926. It would restore the faith of the working class in itself, rekindle the militant spirit of 1925, and make possible the great mobilization of forces which the situation demands.

The organizational measures which would flow from such a political regeneration are as clear and definite as the issues which are at stake. The Labour Party, the Trade Unions and the Co-operative Movement would establish at the centre and in every locality a three-fold alliance as the basis for drawing together every working-class organization nationally and locally for concerted action in the fight for socialism. The details of the plans of action would be worked out on the basis of the rich experiences we have surveyed – of 1920 when the Labour Movement stopped the war on the Soviets, of 1925 and the mobilization of the workers for Red Friday, of the General Strike of 1926, of the elections of recent times and the lessons of the failures of the German working-class movement to stop the triumph of Hitlerism.

All these experiences proclaim in no uncertain fashion that the struggle is not confined to parliamentary elections but embraces every form of mass activity which has characterized the history of the working-class struggle. It is significant that every great advance in the Labour vote has followed closely on the heels of great strike movements. To so mobilize the workers that they will be ready to use their power is the surest guarantee of readiness to vote when elections come, to remove obstructions to elections when obstructions are put in the way, to strengthen the hands of labour representation when elected, to advance from defensive actions to the workers' offensive for socialism and to lay the foundations of a higher workers' democracy when the fight for power has been won.

It will be argued by many that the issues have been correctly stated and that the proposals are good but the Labour leaders will not adopt them. The question of the leadership of the Labour Movement is indisputably the question of questions to which this survey of working-class history leads, and upon which the fate of socialism in this country depends. Almost every page of this book reveals the continuous hammering of the class war against the reformist tendencies of the movement. The class war has proceeded relentlessly. It has produced an independent organized working-class movement, but at no stage has this movement yet produced a permanent leadership with a policy and vision consistent with working-class independence and consistent with its struggles and its tasks.

It is a striking fact of its history that in all mass actions, the great strikes and demonstrations, the workers have turned a willing ear to the Left leaders, and to the revolutionaries. It is equally striking that rarely have the revolutionaries been elected to the permanent posts of leadership in the trade unions, the Labour Party and the Co-operatives; and in some cases where they have been elected they have been rapidly absorbed into the mass of reformism which has marked the leadership. In the great majority of cases those who are elected to leading positions deplore the struggles and view their jobs entirely as administrative posts. Hence it cannot be a matter of surprise that time and again struggles have been thrust upon them without adequate preparation, often indeed, without any preparation at all.

It is important to recognize the cause of this apparently strange contradiction. First there are historical reasons. The Trade Unions and the Co-operatives grew in a period when revolutionary socialism was almost non-existent, when the workers themselves were 'capitalist minded'. The Labour Party grew out of the trade union movement, All the ideology of this period before the crisis of capitalism was carried forward into the period of crisis with a minimum of theoretical discussion. Hence there was not only a lack of appreciation of the character of the crisis when it came but a definitely powerful prejudice against revolutionary Marxism which foreshadowed and diagnosed the crisis. It was thus inevitable that the full realization of the new situation and its lessons should only be learned through bitter experience and disillusionment.

But there have been other important contributory factors, not the least of which has been the policy of self-isolation pursued by the revolutionaries right from the rebirth of revolutionary socialism in the '80's of the nineteenth century. This record shows the S.D.F., the S.L.P., the syndicalists, the shop stewards, and the Communist Party, pursuing a sectarian policy which has left them only on the fringe of the working-class movement. The S.D.F. resigned from the Labour Representation Committee. The S.L.P. refused to have anything to do with the Labour Party. The syndicalists stood aside from 'politics'. The shop stewards refused to stand for official positions in the unions. The communists formed a separate party as an alternative to the Labour Party when the masses were moving towards the Labour Party and not away from it. Instead, therefore, of increasing the revolutionary influence they have persistently been working against the tide of the working class itself and thereby strengthened the influence of the Right who have turned the criticism of policy into an attack upon the Labour Movement itself. Hence only in great moments of struggle which of themselves generate revolutionary opinions has the influence of the revolutionaries spread. When the critical stages have passed and the fervour of the struggle has receded then they have lost ground again and still remain isolated sects.

Still further factors retarding the growth of revolutionary leadership are inherent within the Labour Movement itself. The elections for office both in the trades unions and the Labour Party have taken place invariably when no great actions of the masses were afoot. The revolutionaries who were not outside the Labour Movement carried on no persistent organized campaign for their nominees. At the same time the workers generally thought little of policy and more of administration, whilst the revolutionaries themselves had created the impression of being 'men in a hurry' seeking and expecting an immediate upheaval as a short cut to their goal, 'mistaking the second month of pregnancy for the ninth'.

Candidates at selection conferences have found that the size of their financial backing has often proved a much more important factor in their selection than their record as fighters for socialism.

Thus, all the weight of tradition, of vested interest, of inertia, of administrative habit, and ineffective challenge from within the movement have retarded and stifled the development of revolutionary leadership. This is why the class war has driven the Labour Movement along the path of mass struggles and independence *in spite of its leaders*, and thrust it into a crisis from which there can be no turning back, with a leadership as yet unprepared for the mighty task which lies before it.

To make the necessary changes in the leadership of the Labour Movement from bottom to top is thus the all-important issue in the race between socialism and fascism. Unless this question is settled then socialism cannot win the race. The Movement may have the finest programme imaginable but without a leadership inspired with the will to dare to operate it, whether it be through Parliament or otherwise as circumstances will determine, there can be no victory for socialism.

Can the necessary changes be made in time? Already some leaders have changed their views and openly declare for revolutionary socialism. Others are changing. It is certain that as the crisis grows and more and more of the trade union and Labour Party leaders see that not one of the programmes of their unions is realizable without the working class achieves power and starts to operate fundamental socialist measures, they will also change their views. To rule out such a possibility and probability is to declare that all things in the universe change except labour leaders. It is possible that some will change for the worse and become fascists.

But the great change that is necessary can only come provided that the mass movement for the socialist offensive can be generated in the fight against fascism and war. This change is not a mere formal change waiting upon new internal elections in the Labour Movement. Formal changes will follow in the track of mass activity rather than precede it. Only by the mass concentration of all the organizations of the Labour Movement, both national and local, upon these purposes, only by the actions which follow from such concentration, will the workers be able to see their leaders in the light of present needs and change them accordingly. This is the affirmative answer to the question: 'Can the necessary changes be made in time?' This is how the workers must complete their Preparations for Power. To help in this direction is the purpose of this book.

FOREWORD TO THE 1934 EDITION

The Great War and the years that have followed, seem so much a new epoch in our history, that we are apt to overlook the essential continuity of the development of the working-class movement in this country. The booming 'prosperity' of the war years with their high wages and absence of unemployment were signalized by an apparent access of strength to the working-class organizations, political and industrial. The trade unions grew greatly in membership and influence and the Labour Party membership rose rapidly from a small ineffective group in the House of Commons to a position of power as a governing party.

The depression which has inevitably followed by the law of capitalist economics, has had its influence upon trades unionism and the Labour Party, and if under capitalism a fresh boom is encountered it will no doubt, in its turn, have a reaction upon the apparent strength of the working-class movement.

But these are surface phenomena which give no index to the growth of real socialism. The great majority of those who join trades unions in times of prosperity and leave them in times of depression have no political convictions, and the same may be said for many who vote for the Labour Party actuated by discontent with the achievements of other parties.

Behind these fluctuations in strength lies a steady growth and development of socialism, a growth which is sometimes accelerated and sometimes retarded, but which has been continuous since the days of the pioneers of the movement. This development has not only been in numbers. There has, too, been a gradual elaboration of the practical problems of socialism and of the manner in which the transition from capitalism to socialism may be carried through.

It is natural that in the early days of political representation of the working classes, the coming of socialism was looked upon as something to be aimed at in the distant future. The present was the time to press capitalism for such concessions as it could afford to give the workers. In the result the political activities of the movement were largely devoted to dealing with day to day problems in a capitalist state, and the elaboration of programmes for a transition to socialism were not thought to be of immediate moment. It is in the post-war period that the movement has begun to realize the necessity for planning the ways and means of changing our economic system. This necessity has been sharply emphasized by the wave of reaction that is sweeping the world, a symptom of the acute crisis of capitalism, which is seeking by any means to retain its hold on the economic power of the world.

Throughout the period with which this book deals, councils have been divided, as to the means to be adopted for effecting the change over to socialism. The ultimate aim of the classless society owning and controlling all the means of production has been a common factor amongst all schools of socialists, but sometimes as a distant and almost utopian goal, sometimes as an immediate object to be brought about by violent expropriation.

Although advocates of violence in one form or another have never been lacking, they have singularly failed to make any extensive appeal to the masses of the workers. The salary and wage earners of this country have so far pinned their faith upon the efficacy of industrial and political action. The strike has been the great weapon of the workers from the earliest times down to the present moment, when they had little or no representation in Parliament. The history of the shop stewards, which is dealt with in detail and with full knowledge in the present book, demonstrates how powerful industrial action can be in times of national stress and when unemployment is absent.

There is no doubt that in 1924 and again in 1929, many of the workers believed that they had at last within their grasp the political weapon by which they were to win their independence, and by which the long-talked-of transition to socialism might be accomplished.

It is not necessary here to explore the many reasons why nothing was accomplished in the direction of transition by either of the Labour Governments, but it is beyond doubt that in the result a temporary impetus was given towards the belief that nothing could be accomplished by Parliamentary means. Although the advocates of violence sought to take what advantage they could from this feeling of apathy and despair, they met with little success. The working-class movement remained fundamentally democratic in their beliefs.

There still remain three opinions as to the way in which the transition may be carried through. There are those who believe that violence alone can effect the change, but their numbers are small and their influence is not great. The main body of the working-class movement is in doubt between two other methods. The use of all constitutional powers to their full to effect as rapid a change as possible, trusting to the determination of the workers to exercise their political power to overcome the economic power of their opponents; or the gradual change by imperceptible degrees over a long period of years, with as little disturbance and trouble as possible.

Most of those who are in favour of the first alternative believe that the second is no alternative, as it is an impossibility. A socialist government is not equipped with the necessary influence and economic backing to govern a capitalist state. As soon as difficulties arise, as they did in 1931, and as they must if socialists try to get the maximum of concessions out of capitalism, the government is bound to fall.

The Labour Party will have to come to a definite conclusion upon this issue at no very distant date, because upon that decision their political future will to a large extent depend. It is an issue of gravity and difficulty, and in order that a decision may be arrived at, it is necessary that as many people as possible should concentrate upon its solution.

The opponents of the present National Government may be divided politically into three broad classes. The first of these is composed of convinced socialists who believe that capitalism is economically unsound and that no solution for our present evils can be discovered within our existing economic system. They believe that it is vitally necessary for the salvation of the country to bring about the transition to socialism, and that this can be done by a full use of the constitutional powers of the workers. They are not concerned to preserve all the details of parliamentarism as it at present exists, but rather desire to develop a new and more efficient parliamentary government suitable to a socialist democracy.

The second class, alarmed at the possibility of fascism and alarmed too at the difficulties that will arise in a transition to socialism, cling tenaciously to our existing parliamentary forms, as the one apparently stable element in an otherwise unstable world.

The third class consist of humanitarian, radically minded and peace loving elements who are not opposed to the private ownership of property, but believe that a great deal of ameliorative work may still be done within capitalism. This class definitely insist upon the preservation of all the incidents of nineteenth-century Liberal democracy and are frankly opposed to socialism, as soon as there is any prospect of its being brought about in the near future.

The first class, though perhaps not so great numerically, is important in that it contains the younger members and many of the keenest workers in the movement. It is members of this class that are liable to be led away by the promise of action by the fascists or communists. The third class are prepared to give a qualified consent to a very moderate gradualist policy which leaves socialism as a far off goal. It is largely to attract this class that the gradualist stresses the necessity for moderation and slow change.

It is questionable whether these three classes of people could ever combine to give whole-hearted support to a single government. It seems impossible that socialism will ever be brought into being with the help of the non-socialists of the third class, and it is therefore, I believe, waste of time for those who desire socialism to pander to the supposed wishes of that part of the electorate.

If the Labour Party loses their support by a vigorous and definite programme of socialism, it will take longer to achieve power. This, I believe, is far better than forming a government with the support of persons who definitely are not socialists.

FOREWORD

In weighing up the pros and cons of this difficulty, it is essential to have a clear view of the past history of the socialist movement in this country. It is for that reason that I commend this book to the public. The author is a trades unionist who took an active and leading part in the shop stewards' movement during the war, and who later gave his adherence to the Communist Party. It is in the light of his own review of the historical development of socialism in this country that he has abandoned the belief in the inevitability of violent revolution in this country, and put in its place a conviction that the change can be accomplished by political and industrial action.

That the next great era of world development will be upon the basis of socialist co-operation is, I believe, certain. The grave question we are now called upon to face is, how long the present period of reaction will last. The decision on that question is largely in our own hands and if we have the courage to embark quickly on the new era, we may save decades of suffering to millions of our fellow men.

The study of this book should help many people who are doubtful as to the course to be pursued to make up their minds one way or the other decisively. Decision in the electorate is essential, for if apathy and indecision persist nothing can save democracy in this country from the fate that has befallen it in so many others.

STAFFORD CRIPPS

INDEX

INDEX

INDEX

INDEX